Acclaim for
*Oral Sex Is The New Goodnight Kiss*

"The latest teen-sex tempest in a tube top centers on Sharlene Azam, a Canadian journalist. Packaged with the provocatively titled tome is a documentary by the same name revealing, in the words of "*Good Morning America*"'s Robin Roberts, "what your kids could be doing without your knowledge."

*- Salon.com*

"Over four years, Ms. Azam tracked her subjects down through news stories, reaching them through school principals, counselors and their arresting officers. The book is a series of interviews with the girls, their mothers, vice cops and pimps, as well as brazen teenaged women who recruit more inexperienced girls into prostitution from their communities."

*- Globe and Mail*

"Worlds away from the poverty, neglect and drug abuse that are the hallmarks of prostitution, teenagers who appear bright and well-adjusted are prostituting themselves without batting an eyelash."

*- Toronto Star*

"A revealing read."   *- Metro News*

"Child-sex parties are very real, frighteningly common and taking place in a neighborhood like yours. Somewhere in the city, children as young as 11 and 12 are gathering in basements and playing intricate, graphic sex games."

*- Edmonton Sun*

"Sharlene Azam's documentary and book has the West waking up to a shocking reality."

*- Bangalore Mirror*

# ORAL SEX
# is the new GOODNIGHT KISS

ALSO BY SHARLENE AZAM

*Rebel, Rogue, Mischievous Babe*
*stories about being a powerful girl* (Harper Collins 2001)

# ORAL SEX
# is the new GOODNIGHT KISS
## The sexual bullying of teenage girls

sharlene azam

*Dedicated to my father (1929–2004)*
*and my mother.*

# Contents

# Acknowledgements

I am deeply indebted to the many young women and their families who shared their experiences with me. There were many counselors and teachers who guided me during my research. I am grateful to Joy Katzko, Catherine Williams-Jones, Joy Becker, and Sue Howard. Sergeant Detective Doug Lang of the Vancouver Vice Unit and Detective Randy Wickins of the Edmonton Vice Unit were very supportive of this endeavor and helpful in every way. Sheyfali Saujani, Rona Maynard, Bruce Griffin provided excellent notes. Gali Kronenberg graciously edited the back cover text. Marianne Angelo, designer extraordinaire, is responsible for the fabulous cover and the inside layout. Shane Azam filmed many of the girls who participated in the documentary on this same subject.

I am very grateful to Naseer Hashim for being there every step of the way.

# Prologue

This book is about the growing phenomenon of middle-class girls trading sex for money, drugs and luxury goods and why they do it. "I can work at KFC and make 100 bucks a week, or I can make 400 a night for sex," Lauren, 15, explained. Lauren was part of an Edmonton, Alberta high school prostitution ring – one involving over 50 girls.

Curious to learn how girls who attend school and live at home are lured into the sex trade, I interviewed teachers and counselors at schools across Canada.

I discovered that school girls are working as "recruiters" in exchange for money or drugs. They befriend girls at their school then introduce them to pimps.[1]

[1]Lopez, Rebecca. "Teen Pimp lures girls into illegal sex," WFAA-TV, Mar. 24, 2008. http://www.wfaa.com/video/news8-index.html?nvid=229796&noad=yes&shu=1

[2]Smalley, Suzanne. Contreras, Joseph. Childress, Sarah. Bailey, Holly. Sinderbrand, Rebecca. "This Could Be Your Kid"; Law enforcement is on alert: teen prostitution is flourishing nationwide. The girls are younger, the trade is more violent--and, increasingly, the teenagers come from middle-class homes. *Newsweek*, 18 Aug. 2003.

Although some experts claim "a tremendous increase in kids from middle-class backgrounds who have not suffered mental, sexual or physical abuse who are turning to prostitution to make some extra money,"[2] all of the girls I know who have prostituted themselves have been sexually assaulted by boys they know.[3]

Sexual assault among middle class girls is underreported. "A growing number of teenage girls view sexual harassment and even assault as normal," explains Gerry Connelly, a Toronto School Board official.[4] "Sexual assault and sexual harassment is occurring at alarming rates."[5]

Although recent reports have highlighted the pervasive problem of sexual assault against girls and young women at schools across Canada, no one knows what happens to girls who have been sexually bullied throughout elementary and high school.

The sexual bullying of middle-class girls causes them to be labeled by their peers as sexual objects, making them vulnerable to recruiters and paid sex. "These young girls think, 'I may as well get paid for something that I am already doing,'" explains Edmonton Detective Randy Wickins. Wickins was responsible for the bust of a high school prostitution ring.

What compelled me to write this book was the realization that this is rapidly becoming a middle-class problem. "22 percent of youth involved in prostitution were seeking to earn money not for survival but to purchase "luxury" items (i.e., nicer clothing, jewelry, electronic gear or to support their drug habits)."[6] We are following a dangerous trend already entrenched in other idustrialized nations like Japan where 1 in 20 high school girls has been paid for sex.[7]

When a 12 or 13-year old is happy to trade a sex act for a new sweater or a CD, it speaks to the value in our culture placed on material goods, our

---

[3]"Studies suggest that up to two-thirds of prostitutes have been sexually abused as girls, a majority have drug dependencies or mental illnesses, one-third have been threatened with death by pimps, and almost half have attempted suicide." Kristoff, Nicolas. "Do As He Said." *The New York Times*, 13 Mar. 2008. Editorial, OP-ED Columnist, p. A25.

[4]Alcoba, Natalie. "Girls accept sexual assault as 'way it is,' educator says; team appointed," *National Post*, 22 Feb. 2008.

[5]*The Road To Health: A Final Report on School Safety.* School Community Safety Advisory Panel. Jan. 2008.

[6]*The Commercial Sexual Exploitation of Children in the U. S., Canada and Mexico.* Richard J. Estes and Neil Alan Weiner. The report was issued in 2001 by the National Association of Social Work and the University of Pennsylvania School of Social Work.

[7]Fulford, Benjamin. "Teachers punished in record numbers (in Tokyo)." *South China Morning Post* 22 Nov. 1997

"luxury fever," and simultaneously to the devaluing of sexual intimacy. When girls locate their power so deeply in their sexuality, and yet value it so little, we have to ask why they do not seem to see the value in their skills, strengths, and accomplishments.

Some of the prettiest girls from the most successful families are prostituting themselves. They are being targeted at their schools and at malls—places we consider safe. And, the predator is often an acquaintance.

Not all teens are having sex and, certainly, not all teens are having sex for money. However, the attitudes and behaviors that led these girls to trade sex for money or drugs are shared by many teens.

When a young girl's beliefs about relationships are influenced by pornography; when her online friends decide if she is "hot or not"; when a girl's ideas about her lifestyle and how she should be treated are derived from MTV; when the magazines she reads feature stories about collagen shots for "G-spot amplification"; when her mother takes pole dancing lessons to unleash her "inner stripper"; and her father watches *Naked News* on his mobile, being objectified seems normal.

Given that purchasing power bestows status and materialism is a virtue, it is obvious that girls would want something in exchange for having to imitate porn stars.

Many of the girls in this book are minors connected to news reports about middle-class teen prostitution. I contacted them by writing to their school principals, counselors or the arresting officers.

I asked to interview them because we never hear girls' side of the events. I spent time with them at their homes and with their families. I spoke with their siblings and their parents to learn more about them. The girls tell their stories in their own voices.

The biggest surprise was their parents' complicity. They witnessed their daughters coming home with new clothing, jewelry, and pockets full of cash, but often did nothing.

These parents feel powerless to change their daughters' behavior because they have surrendered their authority to pop culture, celebrities and the Internet. When you learn your 12-year-old daughter has lost her virginity, it is something most parents can eventually cope with and accept. When you learn your 12-year-old daughter has willingly traded her virginity for $3000, where do you go from there?

All of the girls in this book who have had sex with men for money, drugs or merchandise are nice girls, pretty girls, from good neighborhoods—girls who could be your own daughters, nieces, sisters, friends, neighbors.

## ORAL SEX is the new GOODNIGHT KISS

"At one school, students formed a barrier on either side of a narrow hallway to prevent teachers from walking through. In the middle, 12-year-old girls were giving blowjobs to boys," explains Joy Becker, Director of Education for Options for Healthy Sexuality (formerly Planned Parenthood).

12-and 14-year-old campers in Ottawa made headlines when they were found having group oral sex.[8] Counselors assumed the kids were playing cards in a nearby cabin. "Camps reflect what is happening in society," says Dan Offord, executive director of Christie Lake Camp, adding that, "Childcare workers are being caught off guard by the fact that children are engaging in sexual activity. I think parents are also in denial about their children having sex."

It would be easy to believe that these girls and boys are an anomaly, but for this generation, oral sex is like kissing was to their parents.

At Lord Byng in Vancouver, the principal asked Joy Becker and Hannah Varto, a sexual assault nurse, to counsel 4 grade 8 girls who were discovered performing oral sex at school, along with the boys, and the parents.

"The girls were in the boys' bathroom on their knees in a cubicle with urine on the floor," Varto explained. "Or, the boy would stand over them as they sat on the toilet. They described the feeling of being gagged and choked because the boy was on top."

I met Rita and Crystal (names changed), 2 of the Lord Byng students who were involved. Dressed in T-shirts and skinny jeans, wearing loads of eyeliner and clear gloss, they carry colorful Guess? purses.

*Why did you do it?*

"Everybody does it," Rita says

*At school?*

"Oral is not even like a question any more: guys want it all the time," says Crystal, fishing in her purse for her cell phone.

"The girls told us that they loved the attention the boys would give them, which at first was very positive," Varto explained, adding, "The boys would make them feel beautiful, loved, sexy and cared for and that's what they were really needing."

*"Was it worth it?"*

"After each experience, I think, 'Was that really what I wanted, or was it because I was feeling lonely?' I'll look back on some experiences and think, 'It wasn't worth it. I didn't get anything out of it.' There are a lot of different moments you get caught up in, and a lot happens at parties.[9] I think if you have a spot or hole that needs to be filled, sex can replace it. I'm not saying it's one of the righter choices," Rita says.

*Did the boys reciprocate?*

"No," Rita says flatly.

---

[8]"Kids have oral sex at summer camp." *Montreal Gazette,* 4 July 2003, P. A12.

[9]"Grade 9 girls were the group most likely to say, 'They first had sex because they got carried away,'" Council of Ministers of Education. 2003. *Canadian Youth, Sexual Health and HIV/AIDS Study.*

*Do they ever reciprocate?*

"9 times out of 10, if you walk into a room [at a party] you'll see a girl on her knees. But you never see a guy on top of a girl eating her out. It just doesn't usually happen," Crystal explains.

"If it does happen, it's after you leave the party, and only if you're in a relationship. And then, he might do it sometimes really quickly so he can say, 'I ate you out.' But it's not like they're really into it for pleasure. It's just for 2 seconds so they can make you feel like you should give something back," Rita adds.

*Why hook up when it is so dissatisfying?*

"Oral is a chore. It's not the greatest thing, but you don't have to think about it the way you do with sex," Rita says.

*How often have you had sex?*

"With a girl or a guy?" Crystal asks.

"How about a vibrator?" Rita asks laughing. "The only thing that kept me and my last boyfriend together is my vibrator."

*Did you have a boyfriend at the time of the incident in the boys' bathroom?*

"No," Rita says softly.

"Being in a relationship is hard because every guy is a player with you and 6 other girls behind your back," adds Crystal.

*How many boys have you had sex with?*

"I've given head to more guys than I've slept with. It's not like I'm a slut. I'm just easy," Crystal says laughing.

"I've only slept with 5 or 6 guys and 2 girls," Rita says.

"From the time I was 12, I've had sex with 8 people, usually leading from alcohol," Crystal explains.

*Would you classify any of those situations as rape?*

"No. I was raped when I was 9 by my babysitter's boyfriend." Crystal explains. "I'm totally fine now," she says, only somewhat convincingly.

"I've been raped twice in one year. Last year," Rita says. "Both times it was guys I knew. Both times I was drunk," she adds.

Rita has not told her parents for fear that they would prevent her from going out at night. Crystal sympathizes. They talk matter-of-factly about sexual bullying and alcohol as a date-rape drug, as though these are just some of the hazards of being a girl. They also talk about alcohol as a crutch to excuse and explain their own behavior. Their definition of "drunk": comatose. Anything less is "tipsy."

Through role-playing, Varto and Becker, learned that the 8th and 9th grade boys pursued the girls relentlessly. "After 3 hours of being followed around the school being told, 'You're so beautiful why won't you give me a blowjob,' the girls gave in," Becker explained.

Boys have long been taught how to get what they want and to "go for it" when it comes to girls, while girls are expected to be the "gatekeepers". This objectifying mentality speaks to a failure by parents to instill in boys the kind of empathy that would translate into a greater degree of caring in their sexual relationships.

After counseling, Becker and Varto say the boys understood that a girl waving or smiling at them, does not mean she wants them, "For them, everything leads to sex," Varto says.

And, the girls realized that they are deserving of respect. "They told us, 'We are better than having our heads pushed down into crotches when we don't want them to be there,'" Becker says.

Although the parents of the boys were surprised their sons were having oral sex at school, they were unwillingly to fault them. "I think a lot of parents think the onus is on the girls' because 'boys will be boys,'" Becker says. The girls' parents were upset and embarrassed by their daughters' involvement, but they did not think their behavior was cause for alarm.

"We've counseled girls who give oral sex to a boy leaving a lipstick rainbow on his penis. If it starts out being one blowjob here or there and then it becomes 5 or 10 in a day, it would be natural to eventually think, 'Well, why don't I just get paid for this? Why shouldn't I just take some money for it or something else that I want?' And it can be that innocent and that's where it starts. Yet, parents and schools have a hard time seeing the link between rainbow parties and being recruited into the sex trade," Becker explains.

## Pros-ti-tot

"Prostitot" is a term coined by youth to describe the 12-and 13-year-old girls who, after school or on weekends, hang out at malls and make themselves available for sex with men in exchange for merchandise.

Kele Redmond, research coordinator at The Women's Network of Prince Edward Island, discovered the term while conducting a study on the sexual health of youth in that province.

"These girls were identified by their peers as 'prostitots' or 'finger puppets' who offer 'pussy candy,'" Redmond explains.

The terms are a pointed reference to the difference in age between the girls and the men they meet. "The people in these communities know who these girls are and men in their 20s are hearing about them and driving in from other districts to find them," she explains.

Amanda, 13, tells me how it works. "At the mall, a guy will come up to you or you'll meet a guy and give him head or whatever, and then he'll give you a T-shirt or something. You might feel bad, but then you'll do it again. It's not prostituting right off the bat." Amanda lists CDs, beer, and a sweatshirt among the gifts she has received.

Maya, 13, is pencil thin and beautiful. Dressed in tight blue jeans and a fitted brown jacket with aqua-colored piping, she carries a clutch purse decorated with pink and white flowers. She says, "One of the guys gave me Chlamydia. He talked me into doing it without a condom."

Not only are some teens nonchalant about having sex, there is a less than private context for it. Maya explains that she had intercourse with an man, in a car with 4 other people watching.

How does somebody become a 'prostitot'? How is a girl identified as a 'prostitot'? Is there a parallel term to describe the men who are having sex with these girls? The teens in the study explained that the derogatory phrase is only used to describe the girls. One young woman said, "The girl is the one who is available. She's the one getting in the truck with a man she hasn't met before."

I am struck by the girls' collusion in what seems like a sexual dystopia; this collusion turns on the idea that oral sex is what girls will do, getting passed around is what girls will endure, and so getting paid is a bonus, rather than an element that further degrades the behavior.

Soon after Redmond began interviewing teens for her report, a story broke in that community that shone a spotlight on the practice of girls providing sexual favors to older guys. Redmond says, "It mirrored what we had been hearing from other girls. The girls who testified in the case said that they didn't feel coerced, in fact, there was a willingness on their part."

The case involved Los Angeles Dodgers' draft pick, Cass Rhynes, who testified in 2003 that 12-and 13-year-old girls regularly performed oral sex on him. Rhynes was in the 12th grade, at the time. In his testimony, he described in detail his sexual escapades with the adolescents Sara and Brittney (names changed).

Rhynes was caught when Annie, Sara's mother, overheard a late-night conversation between Rhynes and her daughter. He was pressuring her to sneak out to meet him.

"I confronted her, and she explained how she had become involved with Cass and his friend, Tyler, over the school year. When I learned their ages, my heart broke for her. This is my little girl who has never even held a boy's hand, and now she's telling me that she had oral sex with 17-and 18-year-old boys. I was outraged," Annie says.

Annie contacted the boys' parents and was told that her daughter must be lying, because their sons would never become sexually involved with such young girls. She called the parents of 15 of the girls Sara claimed were also sexually involved with the boys, but they refused to discuss the issue. She then contacted the school principal. "He told me to keep it 'hush-hush,'" she says. "That's when I decided to call the police and press charges."

As testimony about the girls' willing participation emerged, the community became increasingly angry that 2 girls would attempt to destroy the reputation of a local hero on his way to the big leagues.

Jamie Ballem, Attorney General, at the time, spoke to me about the division in the community. "Some groups are saying, 'Yes, he's guilty, but he's been punished enough by being publicly exposed. He may lose his athletic scholarship.'"

The case garnered a lot of national media attention, but there was never any mention of the negative impact of the extensive coverage on the girls. Although the girls' names were not made public, their identities are known in their city, where the feeling is that girls who "act like boys"– in other words, behave promiscuously — get what they deserve.

Some believe that the girls became sexually involved with Rhynes in a "quest for fame," and so they should not claim to be innocents. Neither of the girls presented themselves as victims. Nor did they want to go to court. Sara's mom pressed charges because the girls are minors.

"There is a lot of discussion about the responsibility of the girls' parents. Where were those girls' parents?" Ballem asks. "A lot of people don't think the courts should be used to decide these issues." Sara, like many of the girls I interviewed, comes from a broken home where her father is absent from her life.

Rhynes was convicted on 2 counts of inciting girls under 14 to touch him for sexual purposes, but the conviction was overturned on appeal. "It seems we have a 2-tiered justice system. One for athletes and another one for the girls who are exploited by them," Annie says.

As a result of our rapidly changing sexual mores, the line between adolescents and adults is blurred. A decade ago, the notion of a 12-year-old giving an 18-year-old, 200-pound, 6-foot athlete oral sex would have enraged most of society and the courts. Today, the girl is vilified and he is back on the field with a lucrative contract.

In her book *It's All the Rage*, Wendy Kaminer writes that we have immodest expectations of justice. "We want people to be either victims or victimizers without recognizing that many of us are both." Kaminer is not writing about cases involving minors, yet her thinking was echoed in editorials that glossed-over the nature of Rhynes's actions.

Reporters described Sara and Brittney as little Lolitas. Rhynes even spoke to reporters about the girls' morality and how much things had changed since he was a kid. "I wasn't even thinking about sex when I was 12," he explained. And yet no one challenged his sexual mores as an 18-year-old. "All the blame is on the girls, as if it's normal for an adult man to want to have sex with 12-year-old girls," Annie says.

Complicating the Cass Rhynes case is the fact that Rhynes falls under the extraordinary protection that is handed out to professional athletes who get caught deviating from the straight and narrow. In *Out of Bounds: Inside the NBA's Culture of Rape, Violence and Crime*, Jeff Benedict explains that when an athlete is accused of sexual assault there are enormous nets that go up around him. "He is a commodity. He's a product. And he's got to be protected."

John Wolf, a Seattle attorney who regularly defends pro-athletes such as Ruben Patterson, the NBA player who was convicted of the attempted rape of the nanny who worked in his home, says, "You have options you don't have in other cases." In that case, Patterson's defense team hired investigators to delve into the nanny's sexual history, and they spent 9 months looking for a way to discredit the nursing school graduate who had been raised in a Christian home. "She had no history of sexual affairs or even an interest in NBA players," Benedict says. "You had, essentially, Snow White. And that's what you need if you're going to bring a successful case against an NBA player."

Increasingly, girls who are victims of sexual exploitation will find there is little incentive to come forward and tell their stories. Girls know that their worth is determined by how they appear to others; they know that fame is more valuable than romance. These are absolutes in our celebrity-obsessed culture. And yet a girl who acts on these messages will be put on the stand and made to feel as though she is in the wrong. The justice system and society, which should protect her, will, in effect, vilify her and the result is that her life will be ruined at the age of 12.

Young girls who willingly trade sex with adult men for handbags or popularity should be treated as victims. Instead, the girls are blamed for the difficulty of not making the charges stick, and the men are absolved of any wrong-doing. Soon the justice system will only be able to protect a girl who is the poster child for a sexual assault victim.

I spoke with Sara on 3 occasions a few weeks after she testified against Cass Rhynes; her mom was present each time. During those meetings, she provided some information about what had happened, but said that she did not feel comfortable telling the full story in front of her mother. With her mother's permission, I taped our interview when we met alone at a restaurant in downtown Charlottetown. Over Kung Pao chicken and noodles, I asked her to tell me how she became involved with Rhynes.

Sara is small with long, curly brown hair and large blue eyes. She looks babyish and is pudgy. She giggles and seems shy. She also does not wear makeup or clothes that are sexy, tight or revealing.

It is hard to understand how a man could find such a young girl sexually appealing. She seems innocent, helpless and powerless, which may have made her a good target.

At the same time, 12-year-old girls like Sara have realized that their sexuality carries power. Girls are plying that power, not for emotional commitment or security or even for pleasure, but for consumer goods, drugs or simply for male approval. To be "chosen" and "valued" by boys – attractive, powerful, older boys, boys with social status is sufficient incentive for girls to barter their sexual power.

## Sara, 12

In grade 6, I attended the Confederation School of the Arts and I was a really responsible student. I always had my work in on time and I was always on time for club meetings. I think I joined every group and every club at our school. I also joined our church choir, because I went to church with my grandmother every weekend. My best subjects at school were language arts and social studies, but I did well in all of my classes, except math, where I had to use my calculator key chain most of the time.

My routine after school was the same every single day. I was on a schedule that my mom made for me. I would come home and do my homework first, then I'd eat, and then I'd go play.

My home isn't walking distance to any stores, and there are only a few people my age in the neighborhood. I would have been close to my younger sister anyway, but because there was no one else around we did everything together.

We've lived in the same house forever. I have my own bathroom and a skylight above my bed. At night, I can look at the stars. The posters on my walls are of stars: real stars, not celebrities. I'm into astronomy and the galaxy.

Until the beginning of grade 7, jeans and sweaters were my thing. Mostly, I wore straightleg pants and weird, colorful shirts. My mom shopped for me. Entering grade 7 was a big deal, because it meant being with older people. I decided I wanted to wear stuff that was more stylish, so I started to shop more with my friends and I began buying stuff for myself.

*Sara orders a Pepsi and carefully wipes the top of the can with her napkin before cracking it open.*

I was hanging out with an older crowd and they shared their secrets with me. I started to make friends fast. This was the first year that I didn't join any clubs. It was a new school and I was unfamiliar with everything, so I thought I would give myself time. I also dropped choir. All of a sudden I was too busy with my social life to study. I started doing my homework just before class, or sometimes in class. I just didn't care if my homework got done.

I was 12 and I was one of the cool people. I started doing what every 12-year-old did, and maybe what every 15-year-old was doing. I began hanging out with a big clan of people; there must have been about 20 of us. We weren't all having sex, but I guess you could say we were messing around.

When you're mixing with the grade 8 and 9 students, it's kind of a shock. There's stuff going on everywhere. It hits you all at once, and all of a sudden you have to pick when you want to lose your virginity and what your standards with guys will be. Everyone is doing it or talking about doing it.

I met Cass Rhynes through his friend Tyler who I met in September on the school bus. It was the beginning of grade 7. At first I didn't really know who Tyler was. I'd seen him around because he lived near me, but I never really talked to him. Then a couple times he sat with me and Brittney on the school bus, and then more often. We'd talk and he was nice to us. I thought we were just friends. I guess he took it a different way.

Tyler added us on his MSN buddy list (Hotmail's chat service) and we would talk online a lot. The fact that I was getting attention from a 17-year-old was big. I've never gotten that much attention and not that kind of attention, so it was B-I-G for me.

Then he got into sex talk. At first I thought it was disgusting, but then he kept on asking. He just kept saying, "Do you think you could give me head?" He was pretty blunt about it. After awhile it started to click-in that he wasn't joking.

Then I found out that Brittney, my best friend, had done it with him and 2 of his friends. We met him on the school bus at the same time and she was 12 too. She didn't get called names and stuff and she got so much attention from everybody.

Everybody wanted to know what it was like, even though most of them had done it themselves. She got attention from guys and girls. I wanted the attention too. To have male attention is very big for a girl. You have to have it. You crave it.

Two or 3 months after Brittney did it, Tyler started talking to me more. I started to like him and I thought, "If I do this, more than likely he will want to be around me more." Everyone else was doing it and they weren't getting caught and nobody seemed to care. I figured it was my turn. I thought I was old enough, mature enough. I was only 12, but at the time you could never tell that to me. You could never tell me that I was too young. I thought I was old enough.

*Finished with her plate, she pushes it forward. Sara drops her hands on her lap and twirls the edge of the tablecloth.*

When I did it, I didn't necessarily want to do it. It wasn't my main priority to have oral sex with some random guy, but it was like, "Well, my best friend did it, and if she can do it then I can do it." My first time, it was really weird because I hadn't done anything sexual before. I was terrified. I didn't know what to do. I had to ask him what I was supposed to do. I did it, and after that, he just expected it from both of us. I didn't care about doing it. It wasn't like such a big deal, but after we would make fun of him like, "Oh my God, did you see how curly his hair is down there?" and stuff.

I didn't do it for the acceptance. I was already accepted. I wanted to do something that I wasn't supposed to do. I wanted to be a rebel. I thought this would make me greater and better. I got a rush from being with somebody older who has a car. I thought, "They really must have an interest in me, if they're hanging out with a 12-year-old. They can have any girl they want." But I guess we were just easy to get. It didn't really bother me to do it. It was like nothing.

Tyler started to pass us around to his friends after he had been with us, and that's how me and Cass Rhynes got together. Tyler would ask his friends if they wanted us to give them head and stuff. It was really weird. The first time it happened, I thought, "I'll do it once and then I won't do it again." But, I started to really like Cass, and he kept asking, and I kept going.

*On October 22, 2003, Cass Rhynes, 18, was convicted of sex crimes involving the underage girls and sentenced to 45 days in jail. Convicted on 2 counts of inciting girls under the age of 14 to touch him for sexual purposes, he was placed on 1 year probation and required to complete 100 hours of community service.*

One time, there were 5 of us in the car and Tyler wanted his friend, Brian, to do stuff with Brittney. She didn't want to, and Brian didn't really want to, but just to shut Tyler up Brian let Brittney give him head.

*Charlottetown has few community centers. Teens socialize in their cars.*

Tyler was the ringleader. Whenever his friends would be around he'd ask them if they wanted to do anything with us. He'd be like, "Do you want a piece?" He plays hockey and he would tell the other guys, "I know these 2 girls and they're really hot and they'll give you a blowjob." We went along with it because we just thought these guys were so cool and so hot.

There were some guys on the hockey team who didn't approve of what Tyler was doing because of our age and stuff. One guy told us we were hot and that he'd probably watch, but that he wouldn't do anything with us because he didn't want to mess around with 12-year-olds.

They also had this game of points. If you got a young girl you got a lot of points, if you got a fat girl you got a lot of points, if you got a hot girl you got a lot of points. But if it was a slut, you didn't get as many points. Oral sex you wouldn't get that many points. If you had anal sex you would get a lot of points. They called all of the girls "Thundersluts" because their hockey team is the Cornwall Thunders. They put money in a jar, and whoever had the most points at the end of the school year would get the money.

We would hook up with Cass mostly through MSN. Cass would ask us if we wanted to "hang out" and then we'd find a way to meet them. He'd meet us at the church near my house, and a couple of times we did it there or in his car. We would do it whenever he wanted it, but we'd have to do a lot of planning to meet them. They always met us somewhere because they knew they couldn't come to one of our houses to pick us up because they didn't want our parents to know. They knew they would get in trouble because we're so young.

*John Mitchell, Cass Rhynes's lawyer, appealed the guilty ruling to the Supreme Court, arguing that Rhynes was a passive participant. The guilty verdict was overturned. Annie, Sara's mother, says, "Most appeals can take up to 2 years to be heard. How did Rhynes get his appeal before the bench in just a few months?"*

It was easier to meet them if I was at Brittney's house, because my curfew would depend on when the hockey game or the movie was over. I never really had a curfew. Or, if I was at my home and we went for a walk — hint, hint — "a walk," we'd say we would be back in an hour.

We usually did it at the church or at a restaurant. We did it a lot at Tyler and Cass's house. One time, we were in his room on his bed and he asked us to both give him head at the same time. We did. We watched TV for like 10 minutes after that and then they dropped us off. I knew I was being used, but it's funny because I didn't stop after that.

I guess we both liked them, so we didn't care that they were doing it with both of us. It was kind of cool to talk to Brittney because she knew what it was like. It would be like, "Did he do this to you? Because he did it to me." "Did he kiss you?" We'd just sit there and make fun of them.

It went on for the whole year until about March. We had no relationship with them at all. We were just there for sex, but we didn't mind because we wanted to spend time with them. Sometimes we talked about why they went for us. It didn't make sense, but for us it was, "There's this baseball star and he wants me and Brittney." It doesn't get much better than that.

*Sara beams at the memory. We leave the restaurant and walk to my hotel. She selects a bag of barbecue-flavored chips from the mini-bar and settles on the bed. I grab a pillow and stretch out near her feet.*

One time Tyler and Cass were having a party. They told us to call to see what time we should come over. We called and they told us it was too crowded at the party, but that they would meet us halfway and then we could hang out. Cass took us to this old motel that is closed down, but it still has beds and stuff in it. Tyler picked Brittney and I went with Cass. Basically, he just took off his pants and it was just like quick, like nothing. Sometimes he would kiss us, but not always.

We knew why they wanted to meet us, but we never knew which one we were going to go with. Tyler always picked. Brittney went with one of them and I went with the other one. Sometimes they would ask for sex, and we would turn them down because we knew that was wrong.

We had oral sex and that was all; they never did it back to us. I was kind of glad because I didn't want Cass to do anything to me, because I thought I would get really attached to him. Other times I would get mad because I thought, "I'm getting nothing out of this. Why am I doing this?" We liked being with them and we thought we were important and we liked the attention, so we kept doing it. I didn't think it was that bad because it's not like I was losing my virginity.

*Sara's mom calls. They chat for a few moments about when she will be finished, and about her plans to attend Playland.*

The night my mom found out, Cass called my house. It was about 10:30 and he and Tyler wanted me to sneak out and meet them. Earlier during the day a friend of mine told me he wanted me to stop seeing Cass, and that if I didn't he wouldn't talk to me anymore because he didn't want to be friends with a slut. I didn't want anyone to call me a slut and I didn't want to lose his friendship, so when Cass called that night I told him that I didn't want to do it anymore. He got really mad at me, so I told him to fuck off and I hung up on him. I didn't know that my mom was listening on the extension. She came upstairs right away and asked me who had called. I lied, but my sister told her everything.

*She pulls a pillow out from under the covers and curls up.*

Before everything happened with me going to court and my mom finding out I was involved with guys, I always wanted to tell her, but I couldn't. We'd argue a lot and she knew something was up because I was always gone to a friend's house or gone somewhere. My mom knew that I was doing something, but she thought it was drugs or smoking or drinking. She didn't think it was sexual, and when she asked I always told her that I wasn't doing any of those things, because I wasn't smoking, drinking, or using drugs, so I wasn't lying to her.

Through the process of going to court and pressing charges, my mom and I have grown a lot closer. I can tell her the majority of stuff now, but I don't tell her everything. I didn't want to go to court. When I was going through the process of preparing to go to court it was really hard. A lot of people called my house the night before I went to testify and left threatening messages.

When I got to court it was easier than I thought it would be because I wasn't lying. Cass was lying. It wasn't all my fault. I do take some of the blame. I shouldn't have done it, but he shouldn't have asked.

*In August 2004, 3 Supreme Court judges ruled that the Crown would have no possibility of success in prosecuting the case against Rhynes any further. Rhynes's scholarship was reinstated; he plays for Connors State in Florida.*

I am disappointed that he won on appeal. I just wish it would all go away so I can get on with my life. I'm more upset that coming forward and talking about it didn't change anything. Our Sex Ed teacher reads us poems about sexuality. She has no clue. It's nice for her to read us this poetry about the emotions, but what's an STD? We are so beyond the stuff they're teaching us.

We thought about moving, but we're not going to. My mom says that people can just keep crossing the street to the other side when they see her coming. She says they're cowards.

*Sara's mom arrives. She takes a seat on the couch and pulls her feet up under her. After a few minutes, Sara slips on her black skater shoes. She had told me that she did not like talking about her personal life in front of her mom, but keeps talking anyway.*

I decided to go back to the same school even though people were pretty harsh to me. People have called me a slut to my face. I've had "slut" written on my locker and teachers don't say or do anything about it. Other people have said it's my fault that Cass won't be able to play baseball. I don't know why they're blaming me, it's not like he was a top draft pick or anything anyway. He was at the bottom. At school, before we pressed charges, the principal told me not to tell anyone and to keep quite. There isn't a single teacher who told me that I did the right thing.

The only people who have given me any support through this are my family. Me and my sister and my mom are a lot closer now as a family. We talk more now. I know that my mom loves me but I think that I needed to hear her say it. Every day now I tell my mom that I love her and she tells me back.

*She smiles shyly at her mom. I walk them down the stairs and out into the cool, dark night, where the absence of city lights makes the stars appear closer and brighter. I ask her about her father.*

My dad lives in Montreal and he called me when this happened and told me that he was really proud of me for going to court. We're not that close, but I was glad he wasn't mad at me.

*We walk to their car and I give Sara a hug. Annie and I make plans to meet the next afternoon.*

## Annie, Sara's mom

Annie is seated in a booth at a coffee shop near her place of work when I arrive to interview her. She has shoulder-length, curly, reddish-brown hair and is dressed in a blue shirt and jeans. She is sipping black coffee. We order rhubarb pie, milkshakes, and split a plate of fries. Annie has a warm demeanor and dark brown eyes.

Everyone blames the girls for what happened, but I want to know why this baseball star wants 12-year-old girls to give him a blowjob. There must be something wrong with him.

I wonder today if I did the right thing by pressing charges. The whole court process was horrible. The justice system failed us in a way. There was no compassion for the fact that my daughter is 12. It's hard to testify, and she was speaking against one of the heroes in the community, a man, someone with family and connections.

Cass got up there (on the stand) and called my daughter a slut. What about him? His parents haven't said one word to me. It's no wonder their son has no morals. During the trial, Sara stood her ground and she told the truth, but I think we need some reform to the justice system and how it treats young girls who are testifying.

Beyond our experience in the courts, the community has turned their back on us. People have called our house and left messages calling her a rat because she let the cat out of the bag. It seems the community is more interested in protecting the men who exploit girls than the girls.

I'm a nurse, and at work, I've had people come up to me and blame me for what happened, saying that I'm not a good mom. Well, all I did is put my child on a school bus. I'm sorry if that was the wrong thing to do.

*She tells me that she has been reprimanded in the press for being a bad mother, but that she does not believe that she acted any differently from other parents.*

I guess I'm just very naïve. I had the sex talk with both of my daughters. We watch *Oprah* and *Dr. Phil*. I knew she was on MSN talking to boys, and when I'd walk in the room the computer would go off. But at the time, I thought this was normal. I thought all kids were doing the same thing. At work, everyone said their kids did the same thing. I thought it was normal.

People believe the girls asked for this. How can a 12-year-old ask for this? She didn't even get anything out of it. Besides, I don't care if she was standing in front of them naked; they were 18 and 17 at the time. They were the adults, and they should have walked away.

These boys are being told that they can get away with anything. There were guys who walked away and others on the hockey team who didn't approve of the girls being passed around to the other boys.

The lack of community support for the girls sends the message that the media's sexualization of girls is okay and acceptable. As a community we do not protect underage girls from being sexually exploited. We are not talking about adult women: these girls are below the age of consent. The law should at least protect minors.

The night that Cass and his friend called, I picked up the phone because I was angry. I wanted to know who was calling Sara at 10 at night when she was supposed to be asleep. I expected to hear a 12-year-old boy's voice, not a mature man's voice telling my daughter to sneak out of the house. I went upstairs when the call ended and asked her who it was. She lied. Then I heard a little voice from across the hall. It was her sister, and she said, "Mom I think some boy is after Sara for sex."

When Sara was in school the next day, I went into her room and found notes from Tyler, one of Cass's friends, that had been sent to her that were very explicit. "Do you have a pink bra?" "Do you have a thong?" She was asked to flash her boobs on the bus. Sara said that she did and wished that she hadn't.

I gathered everything I could find and called Tyler's mom. She denied that her son could ever be involved with someone as young as my daughter. I called the school and Dale McIsaac, the principal, told me, "We'll keep this hush-hush."

I have been told that the school, and specifically Dale, had been made aware of the problem of seniors targeting and sexually bullying juniors on the buses for quite some time, but he refused to address the issue.

Should the juniors and the seniors ride the same bus if this is what is happening? Dale didn't want to discuss that issue either, he just told me not to make any "noise", and so I called the police, which started the whole process. While this was happening, I didn't want Tyler on the bus with Sara. She has to take the bus to get to school. I told the principal and Tyler's parents that I didn't want him near my daughter, but we still had to get a "stay away" order to keep him off of the bus.

When I first learned about this, I really believed that Sara and Brittney were the only ones who had been targeted by these guys. I thought this was an isolated case. I soon learned there were 7 girls in this row, in a 15-mile radius, that the school bus picks up who were being sexually exploited.

Their parents knew their daughters were being exploited; they were all too scared to speak publicly about what these athletes are doing to young girls. Even Brittney's parents wanted to sweep it under the carpet. This was the first time Brittney was ever on the school bus. Her parents usually drove her to school and then picked her up as well. Letting Brittney take the bus was an attempt to help her to come out of her shell.

When I spoke to them, they were outraged, but they didn't want to know too much about it and they didn't want to press charges. A lot of the

MSN chats were saved on Brittney's computer, so that's how she ended up testifying, otherwise it would have just been Sara up there.

There are days when I cannot believe this has happened to my daughter. I still don't understand what the girls got out of servicing these boys. I guess they'll do anything for male attention. Sara hasn't had a father figure in her life. When my husband and I divorced, he didn't make any effort to spend time with the girls.

Sara is not the one who wanted to press charges. According to her, it's happening to all the girls in all the junior high schools. They pass them around. She's with a guy and her friend's with the same guy next week, which blows my mind.

I have always talked to both of my daughters about sex and that is not something I taught them. To me it's just morally wrong, but according to Sara it's quite commonplace. I'm old school. I don't understand how this generation can share boys.

*When the waitress comes by to refill our coffees, Annie hands her the plates and brushes the pie crumbs into a napkin. She tells me that a lot has changed in her home since this experience.*

Now, I am always fearful for her.

# A Poisonous Culture

25 years ago, a balding, middle aged, white man approached a teenage girl at a school play and invited her to model at his hotel room. The girl knew her father would object, so she asked her mom to take her.

They were met in the lobby of the Hotel Vancouver where he told her mother she should wait in the bar, while they went upstairs. Instead of insisting that she accompany her, her mother asked the teenager what she wanted.

He was not thrilled, but he shot several rolls with her mom in the room.

A few weeks later, she received the photos and a note indicating that she was not model material: she was unable to take direction. She understood what he meant: she had worn her mother's modest bathing suit, not a bikini or just her underwear, as directed. And, she refused to peek out from behind the shower curtain or lie on the bed with her legs in the air.

That girl is me. I had allowed myself to be photographed by a complete stranger based on the promise that he could fulfill my fantasy to be gazed upon and admired by the entire world.

But I was not able to sit with my legs spread, and other things he asked me to do, because they were wrong for me. At the time, I had never kissed anyone. I had never been naked in front of anyone. I had never had sex, nor had any of my friends.

Would I do it today if I were 13 and asked to pose topless? Maybe. What has changed is the level of sexual exposure among young girls. Bombarded with images that link a girl's value to her sexual willingness, girls see their role models engaging in graphic behavior or acting like porn stars and being rewarded for it (at least in the short term).

The training starts early, Bratz dolls, manufactured by MGA Entertainment for preteen girls (7-12) "who are mostly into music [and] computers," are "fully articulated fashion dolls that provide hip and trendy alternatives to traditional dolls." According to the manufacturer's website, the dolls "are inspired by modern advertising and computer anime images"; sales neared $100 million in 2001, exerting enormous influence on the body image and focus of the latest generation of girls, a trend that began (and continues) with Mattel's Barbie.

"Things are heatin' up as Chloe takes to the scorchin' sands of Bratz Beach," reads the advertising copy for the "Spring Break" version of the Chloe character doll. "Strolling in the dreamiest bikini around, she's ready for what's sure to be a summer to remember." Chloe comes dressed in a bikini and see-through miniskirt. She sports peroxide-blonde hair and, like all the Bratz dolls, oversized lips and eyes, pencil-thin legs, and a wasp-sized waist.

Paris Hilton, Britney Sears, Jessica Simpson, Christina Aguilera: Anyone who has ever stood in a supermarket checkout line knows that, in addition to conforming to an extremely narrow definition of beauty (identical to that of Bratz dolls), today's female pop icons are sex objects to be alternately exalted, ogled, emulated, critiqued, condemned, pitied, and recycled...ad nauseum. Even the more respected pop stars—those with actual acting or musical talent, like Scarlet Johansson, Keira Knightley, Avril Lavigne, Cheryl Crow—regularly strike clothing-challenged poses in magazines from *Vanity Fair* to *Maxim* to *Playboy*. Paris posed topless for *Vanity Fair's* September 2005 cover. A year later, Scarlet Johansson and Keira Knightley were nude on *Vanity Fair's* February 2006 cover.

With role models like these, immersed in a culture where sexuality is tied to celebrity status and money, girls are conditioned to feel empowered whenever they are the sexual center of attention. "At a party or wherever, to get attention, 2 girls will start kissing and then all of a sudden it's like everyone is looking and all of the attention is on you. It's like you're on fire," explains Emma,16, a high school student.

To maintain that level of attention, many girls are transmitting nude or sexually explicit photos of themselves via cell phone. The practice is called "sexting". "It is a way to become famous at their school because those photos are widely forwarded among students," explains Joy Becker, a youth counselor. "I've seen everything from your basic striptease to sexual acts being performed," explained Detective Brian Marvin, of the FBI Cyber Crime Task Force of Central Ohio.

Girls understand that the most valuable commodities are youth and beauty: both of which they possess. And, they identify as sex objects because being a sex object is about being desirable, getting attention and feeling powerful.

12-year-old Maddison Gabriel made international headlines when she was chosen to be the face of Australia's 2007 Gold Coast Fashion Week. Although Gabriel's agent says she will not model lingerie, photos of her in heavy makeup and bikinis are online. Gabriel's mother, who has been criticized for participating in the sexualization of her daughter has demanded an apology from Australian Prime Minister John Howard who, on a Melbourne radio station, said, "Catapulting girls as young as 12 into something like that is quite outrageous, and I am totally opposed to it."

Gabriel's mother's response: "I believe the Prime Minister is getting very doddery. He does not know exactly what 13-and 14-year-old girls are like."

Advertising and media feed off of each other generating a proliferation of images that are sexual, include nudity or are pornographic. These ads, billboards and shows become guidelines for acceptable teenage social behavior. Sexual imagery is such a normal part of teens' daily lives that, regardless of family pressures, disapproving peers or religious taboos, very young girls are influenced into dressing provocatively, acting sexy and becoming sexually active.[10]

Drunk, underage girls bare their breasts in *Girls Gone Wild* videos.[11] T-shirts for girls read, "Porn Star", "The Rumors Are True" and "I Know What Boys Want" across the chest. Sweat pants have "juicy", "yummy" and "sweet" printed on the backside. The current brand identity for girls is clear: "I am something to be consumed."

In a Coco Chanel ad, Keira Knightley uses a bowler hat to shield her nipples and a man's shirt to barely hide her genitals. "Safe to say she loves her socks" is the tag line for an American Apparel ad with porn star Lauren Phoenix. Abercrombie & Fitch featured a "Group Sex" layout in a Christmas

---

[10]"42 per cent of Internet users ages 10 to 17 had seen online pornography in a recent one-year period." Wolak, Janis. Mitchell, Kimberly. Finkelhor, David. 2007. "Unwanted and Wanted Exposure to Online Pornography in a National Sample of Youth Internet Users" *Pediatrics* (Feb): 119: 247-257.

[11]Joe Francis, founder of the *Girls Gone Wild* videos series was sued in a civil lawsuit in 2003 by 7 women who were minors at the time they were filmed on a beach in Panama City, Florida.

catalogue.

In a recent ad series for a Tom Ford fragrance, a naked model presses the perfume bottle between her breasts (in a classic porn pose) and against her hairless crotch, barely covering her genitals. Victoria's Secret model Marisa Miller poses for the *2008 Sports Illustrated* music issue wearing nothing but an iPod. It is worth noting that in both the Tom Ford ads and the *Sports Illustrated* photos, the models' pubic hair has been completely removed, a grooming practice that is ubiquitous in pornography and that has become increasingly common among young girls and women.

Gail Dines, a professor at Boston's Wheelock College who explores how media images shape gender and racial identities and the role pornography plays in legitimizing violence against women and children, points out that content that was once considered hardcore pornography—images one might find in the pages of *Hustler*, for example--have been successfully mainstreamed by the advertising and music industries. American Apparel has made a multimillion dollar name for itself by shooting young women in gritty, *Hustler*-style poses, and Joe's Jeans billboards are all pornographic in tone.

Soft porn is featured in most music videos. In the "Tip Drill" video Nelly swipes a credit card down woman's rear where in a fraternity house environment, women appear to be having sex with each other and anal sex with multiple partners.

In "Suck My Dick", Lil' Kim raps, "To all my mother-fuckin' gettin' money hoes...Niggas love a hard bitch/ One that get up in a nigga's ass/ Said he'd pay me ten grand just to belly dance/ Cum all on his pants."

The "P.I.M.P." video by 50 Cent and Snoop Dogg has bikini-clad women, with dollar signs hanging from their crotches, on leashes attached to diamond-studded dog collars. *Rolling Stone Magazine* labeled Snoop Dogg "America's Most Loveable Pimp".[12]

In "Double Up", R. Kelly, sings about sleeping with two women, at the same time, who may be related. In the video for "Buy U A Drink", T-Pain tosses bills at a woman as she dances. Another popular T-Pain song is titled, "I'm in Love With A Stripper".

On *Adrenaline Rush 2007*, Twista's hit song is "Pimp Like Me". David Banner's *Mississippi: The Album* was a commercial success due to, "Like A Pimp". Ludacris's *The Red Light* album features, "Pimpin all Over the World".

Boys are being trained to view themselves as pimps or players who are entitled to sex whenever and however they want it and girls are sent the message that they should be available for sex and skilled at it. *Adorable* magazine sent their teen subscribers a sex guide entitled, "99 Naughty Tricks" including tips on French kissing and oral sex. *Seventeen* and *CosmoGirl* magazines regularly offer sex advice, often without mentioning a relationship as the context in which the sexual contact might take place. Sex as recreation, sex as inevitable adolescent experimentation, sex as obsession are so pervasive that the editors of the recently released *True Images: The Bible for Teen Girls* (Zondervan), feel it is essential to discuss oral sex, lesbianism, and "dream" guys alongside the study of scripture.

How To Make Love Like A Porn Star, Tracy Lords' bestseller is a favorite among girls. As is, *One hundred Strokes of the Brush Before Bed*, an autobiographical account, by teen writer Melissa Panarello who loses her virginity, has group sex, sex with a married man, sex with her math tutor, all before her 17th birthday.

In the pre-teen and teen book market, *Gossip Girl, A-List, It Girl* and *Clique* are bestselling series about wealthy teens' sex lives, in which everyone has a Sidekick (marketed as "your lifeline to your social life"); a platinum AmEx; and coke-snorting parents who have extramarital affairs. In these books, where fitting-in is the priority, even sex is about social positioning and status.

Zoe Margolis, the assistant director on *Harry Potter and the Order of the Phoenix*, became famous for *Diary of a Sex Fiend*, her sex blog and book. Margolis is part of a genre Madeline Bunting of *The Guardian* Newspaper calls "Fuck Lit" and includes, *Secret Diary of a Call Girl, Indecent: How I Make It and Fake It as a Girl for Hire, Diary of a Manhattan Call Girl, Confessions of a High-Priced Call Girl* and *The Internet Escort's Handbook*.[13]

*Gossip Girl* has spun over to television, where the show's pilot treats viewers to underage sex in act 1, drinking throughout act 2, and an attempted rape scene in act 3. Other episodes include lingerie sleepover parties and girl-on-girl kissing.

CBS's *Swingtown* is another of the growing number of TV shows about wealthy teens: its first episode features, teens smoking pot and reading pornography; adults popping Quualudes; and a threesome carrying on upstairs while an orgy unfolds downstairs.

The girls on these shows care deeply about being popular and loved. They pay very close attention to the value placed on being "hot," and become addicted to the power that comes from granting or withholding sexual favors. If you want to know just how much things on TV have changed, only 13 years

---

[12] *Rolling Stone Magazine.* December 14, 2006.

[13]Bunting, Madeleine. "Sorry, Billie, but prostitution is not about champagne and silk negligees: The screen adaptation of The Secret Diary of a Call Girl legitimizes a trade that in reality is utterly brutal and misogynistic," *The Guardian,* 8 Oct. 2007.

[14]Bellafante, Gina. "A Teenager In Love (So-Called)," *New York Times,* 28 Oct. 2007.

ago, the show to watch was *My So Called Life* with Claire Danes playing Angela Chase. Each week 9.87 million viewers (more than NBC's *ER* drew last fall) watched "a decidedly middle-class girl whose grievances with the world were confined to an aching crush, the wish that her mother wouldn't insist on well-balanced meals and her belief that social studies ought to be less boring."[14] There was a distinction in the dress, problems and responsibilities between adults and teenagers: Angela wore baggy clothes, little make up and had parents who were present.

## Teenage Recruiters

15-year-old Rachel and 3 of her friends cross the sports field that separates their high school from Okanagan College. It is a few weeks before Halloween in 2005. The grade 10 girls, dressed in faded jeans, tight T-Shirts and thin, worn sweaters with little or no makeup have been offered money for sex.

The college freshmen loitering near a row of vending machines are waiting to take them to the dorms they share. The girls will be paid $20 each for oral and intercourse. There is little time to linger, as the girls must return to school before the end of lunch and the beginning of math class.

These girls have had sex with these and other guys at least a dozen times since September, the first time on a dare. It started when a couple of boys in the 11th grade, who set up the dates, approached them as a joke for some easy money.

The girls and boys attend Kelowna Secondary School. The girls eat chips and ask me questions as I search for tapes and my headphones. They tell me I am too bony. They quiz me about how often I exercise, what I eat, and if I smoke.

They inform me that I have issues with food, exercise, and control. I am unnerved by the speed at which I have been summed up. I retreat behind my gear.

I ask them how the boys convinced them to trade sex for money. Rachael's hair is pulled back in a messy ponytail and she is wearing a maroon hoodie and jeans. She says, "I think there was just an expectation that you will do stuff with them. It's a game for a lot of them. You get passed around. Within 3 or 4 months, I had lost a lot of my old friends and I wasn't close to my family anymore, but I had these new friends. Guys who would say, 'Go sleep with that guy and I'll give you so much,' and I'd do it. I thought they were my friends, but they were just stealing from me."

Rachel performed oral sex for the first time at a party, because she thought it would make her popular. She was 13. She says, "All the cool people from school were there. If you end up doing something with the jocks, the next day you're cool and you can hang out with them. You'll do everything you can to be one of them."

Jeanine's sweats have "yummy" scribbled across the rear. When she was 12, she attended a party at her boyfriend's parents' place. "His dad asked me if I wanted to make some extra money," she says. She started having sex with her boyfriend's father for money that night.

When I ask her if that was her first experience with prostitution, she is taken aback. "I haven't stood out on the corner; I haven't really prostituted. At a party, I might meet a guy and he might say to me and a bunch of my friends … 'Suck me off and I'll give you so much or a free bag of weed.' So I did."

The girls are offended that I described their behavior as prostitution. They prefer to see it as "hooking up" for a one-night stand. Girls rarely seem to name their actions or admit the truth of it, even to  themselves, in part, because they are disengaged from their bodies. Yet they will say, "If I need drugs or if I want a cool pair of jeans, I'll give head for that."

Kelly is 16 and Asian. Unlike the other girls, she has not volunteered any information about herself.

I ask her how she was recruited into prostitution.

I was never recruited, but I have recruited people. I would bring them to my dealer's house. People who were just starting to get into drugs. I'd basically tell my dealer, 'You can have this girl if you give me a gram or something.' He would usually go for it. I would go to a girl and say, 'He wants to smoke some dope with you.' Then I'd sit out in the living room while he was in with the girl.

It is surreal to hear a girl talk about trading another human being for anything, let alone something as insignificant as a few grams of pot.

*How did you convince girls to have sex with your dealer?*

"It was awful. I manipulated them and made them think I was their friend. If they were kicked out of their house, I'd let them stay at my house. I'd share dope with them; they'd share dope with me. I'd get the friend figure going and I'd do everything behind their backs. I guess you could say I was kind of two-faced with them."

*How did you pick your targets?*

"Just weak people—girls who were just starting to experiment with drugs. Even people who didn't even touch the stuff and didn't know what it was. I would say, 'Hey, do you want to try this? It's pretty cool shit.' I got them into prostitution without them knowing. I always gave them my number and told them to call me if they needed drugs or a place to stay. We'd bond somehow into being friends, and then I would trade them for things."

*How many girls did you recruit?*

"10 or 12 girls, I think. They were younger than me. I started when I was 14 or 15. The youngest was 13."

*What did you receive in return?*

"Like I said, I'd give them to my dealer. He'd fuck them and give me dope."

Kelly describes the girls she recruited as "prissy" girls. "You know the type. Their ass has to be a perfect way; their tits have to be a perfect way. The smart ones," she says looking at me slyly. Presumably, my nerdiness would have made me a target. "Well, the smart ones are okay," she says, laughing.

*How did you get the idea to trade girls for drugs?*

"My dealer would say, 'I like your friend. I'd like to fuck her.' I would say, 'Okay.' Then he'd say, 'I'll trade you something for her.' He basically got the idea into my head. I brought the girls over and he kept on doing the same thing. That's how it was. The girl thinks she's getting a deal because my dealer would smoke a bit of dope with her, but not as much as he would give me."

*How did you feel about it?*

"Good. The girls never asked for anything, and if they did, I always had something to give them. Not from myself, from other people. I used people. I used girls. They were like junk to me."

*Why were they were like junk?*
"Fucking bitches. Think their shit don't stink."

Kelly's bitterness is startling.

*What made you stop?*
"I started on heroin and my mom found out, so my dealer went to jail and we moved here. She thought it would help me to move away from everyone, but it got worse because then I got into crystal meth — that shit came into my life and fucked me over."

*Where was your dad?*
"He's useless. When I was 11 I started drinking. He found out and thought that if I did it at home, I'd be safe and supervised. He thought he was doing a good thing. He didn't think I would get addicted or that I'd like it and try other things."

A few weeks after interviewing Kelly, I met, Courtney, another teenage recruiter.

Courtney is skinny with stick straight brown hair that falls to her waist. In blue jeans, a pink tank top, and without a trace of makeup, she appears to be about 12. She is only 5 feet tall and weighs 90 pounds.

Courtney attends an alternative school where she is finishing 12th grade. She is also a volunteer at Douglas Park Elementary School where she teaches girls how to recognize the signs of being recruited.

"A recruiter who was enrolled at the school had approached at least 10 students, one girl was 8," says Tatiana Sean, a youth outreach worker, who helped develop the program. Pimps have enrolled girls in schools to recruit other girls. "They show up with new clothes, jewelry, invitations to party with older guys. They're the bait," Courtney explains.

# Courtney, 16
The first time I met a pimp, I was 12 and hanging out with my best friend at Guilford Mall. This black guy approached us. He told me he could get me free minutes for my cell phone. We actually said, "Don't you think you're a bit old to be talking to us?" He told us, "I hang out with young girls all the time."

He told us he could get us free jewelry and that he could get us into the bars, so I went with him. He bought me minutes for my phone, took me to dinner, got me into clubs, so I thought he was a cool guy. I knew that he would want something in return because nothing is for free.

When I told him I wasn't going to have sex with his friends, he got pushy, but I was like, "I don't even listen to my parents. Why would I listen to you?"

He could see he wouldn't be able to recruit me, so he told me to invite a bunch of friends out to the bar. I would call my friends and ask them if they wanted to go drinking. At 13, everyone wants to go to a bar. He took us to clubs. We were only asked for ID once, and usually he said, "She's with me," and so we always got in, which was so cool.

I started recruiting girls at my school, or I would meet them at the mall. I would tell them, "I know this really cool guy and he wants to take us out for drinks and I don't want to go by myself. Do you want to come? Free drinks."

Or, sometimes I would tell them, "I know this really nice guy. You'd like him. He wants to bring us out and he'll buy us new clothes and get us free jewelry, free everything." This is pretty appealing to most girls. There's nothing available for kids to do, and their parents don't give them a lot of extra money, so it's easy to bring them in.

In prostitution, there is almost always an older guy behind the whole thing. Either they recruit girls themselves or they find someone like me to recruit for them. Men use girls to recruit other girls because you're more comfortable around a girl when you first meet them.

Girls trust other girls, so they don't think anything when you invite them to a party or to the bar. Part of this is strategy. They know that kids are more aware today of the danger of talking to older men and strangers, so they get young girls or guys to recruit for them.

If a pimp is approaching girls at the mall or on his own, he'll observe you. He'll eavesdrop on your conversation and then try to talk to you about something related. Also, not all pimps are male. There are lots of women who are pimps.

I was always smarter than most of my friends, so I knew when guys were watching me and when they were going to approach me. I always knew when I was going to be in danger. I wasn't as gullible as most of my friends, which made me a better recruiter.

Once I was able to bring a girl in, not all pimps provide drugs right away. They try to figure out what kind of person you are. If they think you'll do it without drugs, that's better for them because there's less risk of an addiction. A lot of girls don't need drugs or much persuading. They don't always see that they're exchanging sex for the gifts or clothes they're getting because they want to believe that they like these guys. Most girls just think it's cool to be hanging out with older guys.

If a girl is on the fence about doing it, a pimp might say, "You should try this drug, it's so good. You'll feel like you're flying". They'll do it and they slowly become addicted. You never admit that you're addicted. When I was 13, I began doing speed and Ecstasy. I would always say, "I'm not addicted. I'd never pay for it. I only do it because it's free."

Once a girl is dependent on the relationship and the drugs, the pimp will brainwash her. He might say, "Your parents just want to control your life, that's why they're telling you to stay at home," or "Your parents don't want you around, that's why they're so mean. I'll let you do whatever you want."

He'll comfort her when she fights with her parents. He's different with everybody. But with some girls he's nice until he can get them away from everyone they know, and then he immediately becomes controlling and aggressive.

After a while the pimp started calling my friends directly and taking them out without me. They were impressed by him and flattered because they thought he wanted a relationship with them. All I wanted was the free stuff. I was jealous that they were going out without me, so I stopped hanging out with them. At that point, I had probably recruited 20 or 25 girls. I didn't have a lot of friends when I was younger, so I mostly recruited strangers.

A year after I had stopped talking to these girls, 1 of them by the name of Leanne called me. I told her that I didn't want to talk to her because she had betrayed me by hanging out with the pimp without me. She told me that it wasn't like that and that he had become really aggressive.

She told me she was really scared and that she needed a place to stay. I told her to go home to her parents, but she said she was scared that if she went home her parents would disown her if they found out she had prostituted. I told her to call someone who cares. I couldn't do anything to help her. I couldn't invite her to stay with me. I wasn't an adult.

I bumped into Leanne's brother recently and he told me that she had ended up on Vancouver's east side prostituting and that she had disappeared. He didn't know that I had recruited her, so he just told me about her like she was my friend.

He said his family was afraid she might have been one of the girls picked up by Pickton.[16] When I look back now, I didn't know where these girls would end up.[17]

*Courtney's shoulders droop and she seems genuinely troubled by her role in Leanne's disappearance.*

When I stopped hanging out with that first pimp, I got into other trouble with guys. My best friend Hillary and I would let older guys buy us drinks and we'd have sex with them.

We met a lot of guys through the chatlines. The ads for the dating services run on late-night TV, so we'd see them and call because it's free for girls to call. Me and my friend Hilary would record a message in our mailbox saying we were 2 hot girls looking to have a good time, looking to party.

She was 14 and I was 13, but we said we were older. So, of course, we'd have every guy leave us messages. We'd pick a few guys who sounded good-looking on the phone and meet them at the mall or at McDonalds. They must have known we were young because we told them we didn't have ID to meet at a bar.

At the mall we would pick out the things we wanted. I had more guts back then than I've ever had. I would just say, "I want this. Can you buy it for me?" In return, they expected to sleep with us. Usually I would sleep with them the same day we went to the mall.

We had different guys for different things. If we wanted clothes or shoes, we'd call up certain guys, and if we wanted drugs, or to go out to eat, we'd call other guys. Sometimes we would hang out in the park with a bunch of guys and they would say, "I'll give you 20 bucks to show me your boobs." We did. Guys are pretty blatant. At parties, it's like, "Take off your shirt; I'll give you 20 bucks. Do a strip tease and I'll give you 100 bucks." We'd make a few hundred doing that.

I had this one friend, she wasn't very smart. She was dancing on the table before they told her to take off her clothes, so she didn't make hardly anything, but we were all drunk, so it didn't matter. It was fun. There are a lot

---

[16] Robert William Pickton was convicted of the second-degree murders of 6 women. He is also charged in the deaths of an additional 20 women, many of them from Vancouver's Downtown Eastside. As of December 11, 2007 he has been sentenced to life in prison, with the possibility of parole after 25 years – the longest sentence available under Canadian law. *Canadian Press*

[17] "Mr. Pickton is suspected in the disappearance of 63 women in all, mostly prostitutes…A special team investigating the case found body parts in a freezer, as well as purses and other personal effects later linked to the missing.... Not one body has been found intact, and a wood chipper and Mr. Pickton's pigs are believed to have devoured much of the evidence." Krauss, Clifford. "Mounties Dig Up Body Parts in Serial Killing Case," *New York Times*, 23 Nov. 2002.

of girls stripping on chats who are not getting paid. I've been approached by guys to be on their website, which is basically porn.

My friends and I met a lot of guys who said, "We'll get you coke if you have sex with us." I did. I was 13. I've never had sex with a total stranger, but I did it even though I wasn't always ready to have sex with them because I wanted the drugs or stuff.

We didn't use condoms, but we weren't scared about getting anything. We didn't think about any of the consequences. I was recently diagnosed with abnormal ovarian cysts, which could have been from being with all these guys, or the drugs. I may be infertile.

The doctors told me the infection in my uterus was the kind of thing they've seen in crackheads on the skids, but never in a girl my age.

I didn't stop doing it until I met my current boyfriend. He was the first guy who showed me that he cared about me and he wasn't going to leave me once he'd slept with me.

I want to be a youth worker when I finish high school because I feel really bad for the girls I recruited. I feel bad for their families. I feel bad because I got out and they may not have. I think most of them could have had a decent life. I don't talk to them and I feel bad about that. I don't know where they are and I can't help them.

I interviewed Courtney's mom, Lori, a registered nurse at a tanning salon, where Lori has absorbed 15 minutes of sun every week for the past 3 years. Courtney is seated next to her mother on a chair carved out of a palm tree, eating salt-and-vinegar chips and sipping a soda. She occasionally interrupts and corrects her mother about the events in her life.

## Lori, Courtney's mother

When Courtney was 12, she was in grade 7 and she was a model student. She was on the honor roll. This was around the time when her father and I split up, and so I transferred her to a new school, which is when the problems began.

Courtney became argumentative, obstinate; I want to use the word cheeky. She started to hang out with people who were older than her, and that was not acceptable to me.

The stress of the divorce, moving, and being in a new relationship meant that I wasn't available to her or my other 3 children in the way they needed, but I always knew where she was and if she needed help.

When I learned that she was in trouble at school, I got tougher with her, which may not have been the right thing. The tougher I got, the more she rebelled. We tried to talk but we both have quite hot tempers. We'd fight and, usually, she'd leave and be gone for a few days.

There wasn't much I could do because she would just run away; it would be a constant thing. I realized she was in a lot of trouble the first time I got a call from the police. They told me she was in a stolen vehicle. I picked her up right away. I remember it was in the middle of the night.

*Courtney looks at her mother dumbfounded. "You never picked me up. You never came to get me. Not once."*

*Courtney's mother glares at her.*

My first instinct was to leave her in jail, and sometimes I did, but my motherly instinct usually kicked-in and I would go get her. I would try to talk to her about what she was doing and how dangerous it was and how she was on a downward slide.

I found out Courtney was getting involved with older men and some shady men when she came home and told me she had been on a boat drinking. I tried to explain to her what these older men wanted from her. Being a nurse, you see things. There was nothing that I could do though: I couldn't punish her; I couldn't ground her; I couldn't take things away from her.

She was only 12, but she knew that if I did more than ground her, she could go to the police or social services and report me. I told her that if she wanted to live at home, she had to be part of the family.

Her behavior affected all of us. It was horrible. She has 2 brothers and they have attention deficit quite severely and they didn't get the attention they needed. I also had an 8-month-old baby at the time and I was in a new relationship and it didn't get the attention it needed.

A lot of the time I can remember being really angry and saying, "I love you, but right now I don't like you very much." I used that cliché a lot. When we would fight, I would tell her, "If you don't like it, leave." So that's what she'd do. I think I probably told her that I'd be happy to pack her bags, too.

I've always believed in tough love, and I think to appreciate what you have, you have to know what it's like out there in the cold. I always hoped she wasn't in a huge amount of trouble. Like I said, I always tried to keep an eye out for her. I think I knew where she was most of the time she was gone.

She was on the loose from the time she was 12 until just months ago when she met a boyfriend and moved-in with him. I didn't appreciate that he was a lot older, but again, there was nothing I could do. I'm still trying to put my own life back together. I think he's good for her because she's back in school.

I never knew, until recently, that my daughter was recruiting girls into prostitution. Courtney can be a smooth talker, so I can see how that could happen, but I was not aware that she was recruiting other girls into anything. I didn't think she was harming anyone but herself. I was constantly afraid that I would never see her again. Every time the phone rang, I thought it was the police calling about her.

If I compare myself to Courtney, I was never as wild. I've told her I've had my share of a few beers when I was younger and underage and I dated a few guys in my time, but kids today are so bold. Now I'm worried about her younger brother. He's getting into trouble now with drugs. I asked Courtney to have a talk with him because she's been through it. My son is a really little guy. A lot of men want to have sex with boys, and he looks like he's 9. I told him to be careful with drugs because there are a lot of weirdoes out there.

*Lori asks if we can finish the interview in the tanning room and disappears to change into a robe. She waves me into the room where she is seated on the tanning bed.*

I think overall I was a good mom. My advice to parents is to talk to your kids; try to stay calm; always know where they are. Courtney was a good kid. She came from a good family, but peer pressure was a big problem and hanging out with older kids.

Although she's not easily talked into things, I think she was talked into trying drugs and drinking. I think the best advice I can give parents is to listen. The biggest thing is listening, and maybe I wasn't there to listen. The biggest warning sign was the first time she didn't come home, and after that time I felt I had no control any more.

I think that if Courtney had felt loved, she would not have looked for it outside as much.

*Lori lays flat on the bed and asks me to tell the woman at the counter to hit the button.*

Courtney introduced me to Leigha. They recruited girls together. I met Leigha at the YMCA near her home in Surrey. She is cute and fashionably dressed in a pleated blue miniskirt and pink T-shirt with the phrase "always sweet never sour" written across her chest. She is in her last year of high school. Unlike Courtney, Leigha shows no remorse for the girls she recruited. She also shows a lack of connection to other people and especially to other girls. There are shades of Karla Homolka in her.[18]

Leigha believes that she became a recruiter because her parents were strict and because she was bullied. When I ask her if she knows what happened to the girls she recruited, she tells me that she does not care.

## Leigha, 17

All through elementary I was a geek. I had no friends. I used to cry every day because everyone picked me on. One time I cut my hair myself and everyone made fun of me. I had 1 friend that I hung out with; I was never the girl who got invited to all the birthday parties.

When I was in grade 2, I was told that if I didn't go on Ritalin I would be sent to a special school. I was really hyper. I couldn't sit still in class. I was a bad distraction for the other students. I was on Ritalin for 5 or 6 years. I stopped taking it myself in grade 7. Being on Ritalin only made school worse for me.

Every day at lunch they would announce my name over the PA to come to the office to take my medication. Everyone knew, and it was horrible because they all made fun of me.

In grade 6, when I started doing speed and was taking Ritalin, I didn't eat and I was super skinny. I looked gross. Now I'm 5 feet tall and I weigh 125 pounds or a little more, depending on the day. I love to eat.

I was always really different from the other students. I was also physically smaller. Until grade 5, I wore dresses and pretty little shoes to school every day. Everyone else wore jeans or shorts or casual clothes, but I loved to wear frilly dresses. The dresses made me feel beautiful and feminine. My mom would make them for me, and I always received a dress on my birthday.

My home life was very strict. I was not allowed to have sleepovers because my mom didn't like them. I was also never allowed to have big birthday parties. I was only allowed to have 2 or 3 friends over for my birthday. I also had a bedtime. Not a curfew—a bedtime.

Up until grade 8, I had to be asleep by 9. My parents would make sure my light was off. They were always breathing down my neck.

Grade 8 was my first year in high school, and I was still a geek for

---

[18] Karla Homolka was convicted of helping Paul Bernardo rape and murder teenage girls.

most of that year, until I became friends with a girl who smoked. I started smoking, and that made me feel so cool.

We all wanted to try weed, too, but we didn't know where to get it. And then I started hanging out at the main bus loop by the mall, where I met so many cool people. They didn't pick on me. They thought I was pretty and fun and they treated me like a normal person. At school, I was a freak, but with these people I was totally accepted. These people were much cooler. They didn't have a bedtime.

It was around grade 8 when I met these kids and started using drugs and getting into trouble. I was so sick of my parents. It was too much. These kids could do whatever they wanted. They didn't have a curfew. I started running away from home because my parents were too strict. I wanted to be cool and hang out with an older crowd, the wrong crowd. Everyone was smoking pot and drinking and I thought that was pretty cool. I liked being high.

My parents divorced right around this time and my mom remarried. My relationship with my step dad was great until my brother was born, and then he just stopped paying as much attention to me. When I would fight with my brother, my step dad would just give me $20 to go away and hang out with my friends. He basically paid me to get lost.

My step dad had a really good job and he and my mom would spend so much money. They bought new cars and a boat. They bought so many things. Then he got an offer at an Internet startup and he thought he could make a lot more money, so he left his job.

Money started to get tight and he and my mom would fight a lot. One day, my mom just packed up and left to live with my grandmother. My step dad didn't want anything to do with me, so I didn't know where to go. My grandmother came and got me and I lived with her for about a year.

My mom started working with her friend cleaning houses. She met another guy and now she's living with him and my brother. She didn't really want me, so I stayed at my grandmother's, and this is probably around the time I started recruiting.

I started doing it because during the time I was hanging out at the bus loop, I met some girls who would tell me to hang out with their guy friends. They were trying to recruit me. I told them that I wasn't into that, so they invited me to go around with them to meet other girls that we could bring in.

Then they asked me if I wanted to go to a party downtown. I did. I was Little Miss from the suburbs, so this was, like, awesome. They dressed me up in a pretty dress and some nice shoes. I was like, 'Wow, I'm looking pretty hot!'

They took me downtown, which is about an hour away from my grandma's home, and they tried to put me on the street.

They told me, "This is how we make money, so go make some money for us." I wasn't about to prostitute myself. I flagged down a police officer and told him that I was scared and that I wanted to go home. He drove me home.

When I returned home, the people who took me out there kept calling me to find out what happened. I told them that the police took me home. I didn't tell them that I stopped a police officer or that I wanted to be taken home. I told them I was not going to be put out on the street again. I wasn't going to have sex with any guys.

They told me that I would have to recruit girls or they would beat me up. I didn't have any problem bringing girls to them. I would bring them all of these stupid little girls. I would introduce them to the female pimps and they would go off and I would never see them again. I didn't care too much because it wasn't affecting me. I was getting what I wanted: booze, cigarettes, money for clothes, McDonalds. Plus, I got to hang out with them.

I started actively recruiting girls when I entered high school. It was easy to bring them in and it was better than doing it myself. I got girls that I didn't know very well and that I didn't care about to do it. I didn't think about how it would affect them. I didn't care. If I wanted a pretty shirt, I'd have to bring in a couple girls, and then I also made money from what they made.

I felt awesome about recruiting these girls. I was like, "Yeah! Look at what I did. I got another one." I knew it was bad, but I didn't care. Personally, I couldn't imagine sleeping with somebody for money. I think it's degrading.

Sex should be with somebody you care about. I was good at bringing girls in. I was a good recruiter. I'm obnoxious and stubborn. The girls who are good recruits are usually good girls. They do what they're told.

I would approach different girls, sometimes at school or sometimes at the mall, and I would get to know them. If I found out their family life wasn't great, I would invite them to hang out with us. I would tell them that we had so much fun and that we could get them money. Whatever they needed, I would tell them that I could help them get that specific thing.

They would get free stuff for a while, and after they were dependent on the relationship, they were told that they had to do stuff in return. They would tell the guys, "We don't have anything to give you, except our clothes," and the guys would say, "Why don't you give us a little blowjob?"

Then slowly they would get passed around, and then, depending on their situation, they might end up getting invited to parties and passed around that way, or working out of someone's apartment after school.

I don't think all of the girls I recruited ended up being hookers, prostitutes, or sluts. A lot of girls became recruiters and ended up doing what I was doing. But I don't know what happened to most of them. I know one girl got out of it, but she was raped and had a child. I know another girl who also got pregnant and has a child; she's still messed up on drugs.

I stopped doing it because my grandmother didn't like that I was getting all this free stuff. She thought that maybe I was selling drugs. She told me that she didn't want to have anything to do with me. She didn't want me in her house.

My biological dad let me move in with him if I went to rehab, because I was using coke and speed, pretty much anything I could get. I did, and I got clean. I've been clean for the past year.

I was never in touch with my real dad before I moved in with him. His mother would drop off clothes or money on my birthday, but I didn't really know him. I moved-in with him because I didn't have anywhere else to go. He's still strict, but it's more in terms of how I present myself. He doesn't like me to drink. He doesn't want me to smell of smoke or alcohol. He doesn't want me to call guys and he doesn't want guys calling the house.

He does like my boyfriend, but he only wants him to come over for Thanksgiving dinner. He doesn't want any guy to spend the night here, but he doesn't mind if I spend the weekend at my boyfriend's place sometimes. He expects me to go to school and to work. As long as I'm good, my dad won't kick me out. If I refuse to go to school or work, he will kick me out.

I have been dating my boyfriend for a year. He takes really good care of me. He's 23. He's a welder. He owns his own home. He owns his own jeep. He's a drummer in a band. He's 3 inches taller than me, so he's a small guy. He loves to ride dirt bikes. I met him at a party. I was dancing with this other chick and he was drinking green-apple vodka and I was so thirsty so I asked for a sip. We work well together sexually.

My mom hardly ever calls me. I feel like she's abandoned me. I'm close to my grandma again. I help her pickle peppers and jam jams and jelly jellies. If she needs a favor, she calls me. I spend 2 nights a week at her place. I call her every single time I have problem. She's really a mom to me.

# Under The Influence

"If I'm with a guy and he says the word 'pussy', I can get completely freaked out. Any words that recall my past and being taken advantage of sexually freak me out. I've done a lot of ecstasy, coke, pot, pharmaceutical drugs. I have a lot of weird, messed-up memories that I can't even relate to," explains Caitlyn, 16.

I met Caitlyn at Nanaimo District High School through Joy Katzko, a drug and alcohol counselor. Joy is currently working at an elementary school with 12-year-old girls – 5th-graders – who strip at parties. "They don't see any problem with it, especially since there is no sex and lots of free alcohol," she explained. "They could easily be talked into stripping for money. An older girl promising an easy 50 or 100 bucks to dance for a few men at a party and they'd be hooked," she says.

Joy who is in her late 50s has worked with teens for over 20 years. She is short with silver hair that has bright purple highlights. To walk down the hallway with Joy is to experience popularity. She knows many of the students by name and a few latch-on for a hug.

Joy has arranged for me to meet Caitlyn and 10 other girls at lunch. They are waiting in the art room, where the shelves are covered in elaborate clay sculptures and the walls are pinned with charcoal drawings.

I open a few bags of chocolate kisses wrapped in silver, pink, and gold foil and ask the girls questions about their neighborhood. Some of them live on nearby Gabriola Island and take the 6:00 a.m. ferry to school. Summering tourists have pushed housing prices on the island into the 7 figure range.

I ask them when they became sexually active. All of the girls started having sex by the age of 12. All of the girls except Jaclin, a pouting blond with a moon-shaped face whose religious parents believe she is still a virgin, are allowed to overnight at their older boyfriends' homes.

Jaclin, who is soft-spoken, says that she took a "virginity pledge" for her parents. She says she is constantly afraid that her mom will find out that she is having sex. "I know that if I were to tell her, she would be really upset and wouldn't accept it. When I turned 13 she said, 'If I find out you've had sex …' that she'd kick me out. That sounds harsh, but she wanted me to know that sex is for marriage." Jaclin has had sex with 5 different boys, at 5 different parties.

The girls are sweet and try to make Jaclin feel better by telling her that boys have casual sex all the time and never think twice about it, so she should not either.

Silvia's hair is parted in the middle. It falls neatly to her shoulders, framing her long, pale face. "I've had sex with people I've just met, without a condom and even before I was on birth control. I've been worried about being pregnant quite a few times."

Caitlyn, who has been winding pesto fettuccini around a plastic fork with her fingers, tells Jaclin, "I've been high and I don't know what I'm doing and I black out. I've had sex without them caring about me and without me knowing them that well. It was just something fun we were going to do and we were safe about it. And it wasn't so much about STDs or pregnancy. It was more like, afterwards, I don't even know them enough to hang out with them. I don't even know who they are as people."

Caitlyn has blue eyes and long, blond, feathered hair. In her flowery skirt and cowboy boots, she is a "vintage" girl. I ask the girls if they have ever traded sex for anything. Blushing, Caitlyn says, "When you're summing up someone's assets, it's not always their personality that's taken into account."

Jennifer says, "With some guys you just know that if you do something with them, you're going to get something … drugs, clothes, a fancy dinner."

Andrea, dressed in a 70s style, red polyester dress and flip-flops says, "If you're hanging out with guys who have drugs and you're not  paying for the drugs, they expect something in return, and if you don't give them that, they're not going to hang out with you anymore because they don't want to waste their money. I think some guys can be pretty harsh".

After our initial meeting at her school, I interviewed Caitlyn 4 times including on Halloween night when she and her friends were getting dressed for a party.

*I ask her how drugs and sex were connected for her.*

"Girls who get into drugs when they're younger get introduced to the sexual world a lot earlier, because the people they're with are older and they have drugs and they have more control over you because you want what they have. You'll do stuff for the drugs, so you progress quicker sexually," she explains.

Caitlyn's twin sister Emma pokes her head in to ask for help putting her hair in hot rollers. Emma is a gorgeous, freckle-faced blond. The summer before she entered high school she shot up 3 inches and her hair grew long. "I couldn't walk down the street without guys hanging out of their cars trying to get me to look at them," she says, smiling sweetly.

At school, the boys in 12th grade showered her with attention: they waited outside her classes; they followed her at lunch; they feigned fainting spells whenever she walked by.

I ask her about the downside to being popular. Emma says, "If you've got looks, you're constantly being offered drugs. Guys will be like, 'Do you want to do a line? Come on, do a line with me.' A good-looking girl at a party is a total victim." She pauses before adding, "Guys love giving girls drugs because it changes them. It drops their shield. It makes them completely ready to do whatever they want: talk, kiss, have sex."

She lists crystal meth, cocaine, Ecstasy, and GHB as the drugs that are readily available at parties. Emma says she takes GHB, the date-rape drug, most weekends. "It makes you feel totally loose." She tells me she uses it to take the edge off of cocaine. "Usually I'll take it if I'm with my boyfriend, but it's not like Ecstasy because you can pass out at any time."

GHB looks like clear Jell-O and is sold in Dixie cups. "It's extremely salty, so you know when you're taking it," Emma says, nervously clicking the fat purple beads around her wrist. "If a guy offers it to you, it's because he wants to get you naked." She tells me it costs about $20, but that she's never paid for drugs. "If a girl got hooked, she'd have no choice but to strip or prostitute."

Caitlyn teeters over to the mirror in the hallway. She pokes long, white feathers into her hair, which is secured in a bun. In her tight, pink satin costume that rides dangerously low, she is every bit the Vegas showgirl. She dances suggestively for us. "I think that pretty girls get pushed into the world of drugs because people have ulterior motives. They notice that when girls are high, they're more fun or wild," she says.

I met Caitlyn again a few weeks later to get a more complete picture of her life.

## Caitlyn, 16

My mom's a biologist and my dad's a geologist. I had a really good childhood and my parents have always been very supportive, but then I hit adolescence. I didn't have problems in my life; I created them. It wasn't anything that I was born into; I was born into a very normal family and I should have just stayed on a normal path, but I didn't.

When I was young I was really protected from media and sexual advertisements. We didn't have a television. I didn't ever read magazines. I read *Narnia* books. Because of my parents' professions, I lead a pretty natural lifestyle.

In grade 7, I was exposed to girls in magazines who were presented in very sexual ways and I started to associate my body more in that way. I got a lot of attention from guys when I dressed a certain way and acted totally crazy. My parents split up right around this time; I stayed in Oak Bay with my dad because my mom travels so much.

Grade 8, I started smoking and hanging out with older guys. They say smoking is a gateway drug because it leads you onto other drugs, which was true for me. My friends from elementary didn't want to try drugs. They were still into art and school, so I moved to this other group and I felt accepted because they were all doing drugs. I started with ecstasy, then I tried coke, pot,

---

[20] "From 2002 through 2006, researchers tracked the smoking habits of 217 sixth graders, whom they recruited from six schools in Massachusetts. Almost one third of kids interviewed who tried smoking said their first cigarette brought them a feeling of relaxation, and two-thirds of those kids became smokers." DiFranza, Joseph. 2007. University of Massachusetts Medical School.

[21] "In a study of 312 Canadian children who were followed from kindergarten up to seventh grade, researchers found that 17 percent said they had sex by the time they were 13 years old. Students who had negative relationships with classmates and teachers had a higher risk of engaging in early sex." Brendgen, Mara., Vitaro, Frank., Doyle, Anna-Beth., Markiewicz, Dorothy., Bukowski, William M. "Same-Sex Peer Relations and Romantic Relationships During Early Adolescence: Interactive Links to Emotional, Behavioral, and Academic Adjustment." 2002. Merrill-Palmer Quarterly 48 (1): 77-103

pharmaceutical drugs and I drank like crazy.[20]

I got all of my drugs from older guys. I used hallucinogenic drugs all the time because I wanted to see the world from a different perspective. I can't remember a whole bunch because I have crazy blackouts from the drugs. I overdosed and ended up in the hospital twice. I remember drinking so much that I would blackout for long periods of time; hanging out with older guys left me vulnerable to sexual abuse when that would happen.[21]

I've always been drawn to new experiences. I like exotic foods and travel, so it just made sense that I would like to try new drugs and new sexual experiences. I like anything high risk, so drugs, sex, meeting new people made life exciting and unpredictable; I never knew what was going to happen next. I loved the excitement of it.

The first time my dad went out of town, I invited 500 people to his house. I had sex with more than one person that night and in the morning I needed to get morning after pills, but I was grounded because my dad was mad at me. I was only 14 at the time. I had to tell my dad that I needed to get these pills. He found out how many people I had had sex with and their ages and freaked out, but he wouldn't talk to me about it. He just wanted to press charges against these guys and put them in jail. He wouldn't talk to me about my emotions, or look at why I would allow men to touch me in that way.

My mother was freaking out too and wanted to send me to rehab. A psychiatrist told my mom, "If she lives to be 20, consider yourself lucky." I think this was also when my dad was diagnosed with Parkinson's Disease.

It was the middle of grade 8 and I had lost most of my old friends and I started to feel isolated from my family. My sister couldn't relate to me and my dad didn't really talk to me because he didn't like the way I was changing. My mom was always open, but she was in South America doing research. I didn't like being at home with my dad because he was always giving me shit, so I'd get stoned before going home and then I started running away. Once I went to Seattle with some guys I didn't even know. Another time, I almost made it to California. Me and my girlfriends partied with the Navy guys.

And then I met a guy at a party who was 21. I was 14 and I had just started grade 9. I started staying at his house. I did a lot of drugs with him and it was quite a sexual relationship.

I think this is when I began to associate my own personal power with giving a man pleasure. I liked hearing them make noises because it made me feel powerful to be able to affect someone in that way. I didn't know I had so much power. I liked having someone direct all his attention at me. Sex made me feel really powerful. It was the first time I felt someone was really under my control. When you see really hard solid men lose their shell, that's really a powerful thing and it is all the time whatever kind of sex it is.

Sex wasn't anything special or anything I was sharing with anyone special. It was a power trip. I didn't care or see any spiritual value in the fact that I was joining my body with another person. I was having sex with all these people because I got a rush from it. I went along with everything they wanted to do because it was just something fun to do or I did it for attention or because that guy has a connection to get you something you want – drugs, clothes, whatever. I've had threesomes at a really young age. I never thought to say no. I didn't think there was any power in saying no.

I've had sex with people that I didn't know. I hardly even knew their names. There was no trust or human emotion. I was joining my body with men that I didn't know well enough to hang out with after. But, I liked doing it. The drugs were a bonus, but that wasn't the only reason I was doing it. I liked the sex.

During that time, I didn't really value my body so much. I wasn't really grounded. My body was more just like something I'd dress up, put in certain clothes and prance around with. My body was for other people. It wasn't so much this is my body, this is my property, don't look at it like that. It was more on display for other people. I think that can happen to a girl when her body feels dirty. You just don't care anymore.

My parents saw what was happening and they were really scared for me. They're really scientific people and they wanted a scientific reason to explain my behavior, so I did see a lot of psychiatrists who always wanted to put me in a mental institution and put me on drugs. They were telling me that the chemistry in my brain was off. They always told me that I had problems, that I was crazy, and that I was hurting people. It was negative reinforcement so I didn't believe I could be a successful person.

I got kicked out of my high school and so I had to go to an alternative school. The principal at the alternative school told my parents that students don't fall through the cracks because there are a lot fewer students, but all of the students in the school are doing drugs, all the girls in the school are very sexually active. There are violent students in the school. They're taking the students who are causing problems in all the high schools and concentrating them into 1 school, which isn't always the best thing.

The first day of school, I met people within the first 10 minutes who were like, "Oh lets go get stoned. Let's leave." So we left, smoked a whole bunch of pot and came back to school stoned the rest of the day.

There was also a lot more influence to be sexual by the girls. A lot of young girls had lots of abortions or had older boyfriends so I felt normal having an older boyfriend, doing a lot of drugs and having sex. You're not really getting an alternate influence other than the teachers. I was still doing drugs and having sex with people in random ways, a year after I started there.

I think that's when I really started to get recruited for people's personal use. I would meet these guys and just go with them. They would be like, "oh just come on this trip".

Then my dad kicked me out of our house because I was sneaking out after everyone was asleep or I would sneak guys into our house. I just thought it was fun, but my dad totally freaked out.

I came home one day after being gone for a few days and there was this letter on the door and all the locks were changed and it just said, "I can't have you living here anymore." I felt abandoned by my family: I was problematic and they weren't going to take me in anymore, which was weird because you just always have that unconditional feeling around your family. I was so upset because it wasn't even an option we had talked about - about me not living at home.

I went to live with my mom after my dad kicked me out and I was really upset about that too because it meant leaving my really good girlfriends. They weren't a good influence on me, but they were my best friends. My mom was living on a remote island and I hated that too. I wanted to be with my friends and just meeting new people and I couldn't do that anymore.

My mom was really good with me. We talked a lot. She told me she was taking me to see one last counselor who was more of a spiritual healer than a psychiatrist. Her name is Marion Roper. She was just like me. She wore long, flowery skirts and she had blonde hair and she laughed a lot. She didn't sit behind a desk and tell me I was the problem. We drank tea and she didn't pretend to be perfect.

Marion taught me how to become whole within myself so that I didn't need attention from a man to feel good and she never told me to change. She made me feel as though I was normal. It's all about feeling normal and I think a lot of the problem with our medical health system and psychiatrists is that they don't make you feel normal.

Feeling like I was normal and capable of doing successful things made me feel more positive about myself and the future and what I could do and that reflects in all sorts of ways too in my life. It made me feel positive again. She made me feel more peaceful and grounded and content and I think that changed a lot of things.

She would always compliment me rather than telling me how I was screwing up stuff or that I was destructive. Marion would always tell me that I was a good person and a nice girl and I started to believe her.

I'm back in a regular high school and I'm getting a lot of citizenship awards and a lot of respect from people and positive energy. I think when I was on the other path I didn't get any positive energy from anyone. I didn't look at my family as though it was a good thing because they always give me shit. Marion cared about me no matter what, which made me feel good, so I put more energy into working with her.

I still shift between not really valuing my body, not minding if I'm with more than one guy and freaking out if a guy even touches me, but it's definitely getting better.

## Wanda, Caitlyn's mom

I'm an endangered species biologist. Being a mother, to be honest, was not the easiest thing in the world for me. I seem to always be struggling to find time for all of my interests since I'm interested in so many things.

Albert, their dad, is a geologist and he and I were together because we both like outdoor things and going off on adventures. We were not together that long before we got married and went off to East Africa. We hadn't discussed having children and then I was pregnant. I returned home to Canada when I was 7 months pregnant and learned I was having twins. We returned to East Africa when the girls were 6 weeks old. We stayed there for a year and then came back to Canada, which was very hard because I didn't have any help.

When the girls were young, I mostly stayed at home. I worked as a naturalist on sailboats on weekends, so I would go off for 10 days to a couple of weeks and my mom would take care of them. I regret that there were times when I was taking care of other people's kids, instead of my own because as a naturalist you take children out into nature.

When the girls were 9 and in elementary , Albert and I separated. We had 2 houses that were a block apart. At age 12, the girls got into partying and boys. Caitlyn started getting a little more out of hand around that time and it was also the time when I had to move away from the girls to another city for a job, so they lived with their dad. I saw the girls on weekends. They really hated the arrangement and would break things when they would come up to see me.

Even with all of our resources, I could never find anything that interested Caitlyn, or that would pique her curiosity. I wanted her to find something that she could care more about than just pleasing herself. During the worst period of Caitlyn's time, which was around age 12, I asked her if she wanted to go to Guatemala with me and so we did that. When I took her there, I think she thought it was going to be like Disneyland or Hawaii, places she had been with her dad. I think it was a really good experience because she saw true poverty.

My daughters have never wanted for anything. As a family, we've never talked about money and it's never been an issue. We've done so many things and been to so many places.

After Guatemala, Caitlyn went to live with her dad again. I remember going to her grade 7 graduation and seeing that she was really seriously getting into partying. It was just a short time after that that her dad phoned me to say that the police had picked her up off of a beach; she was lying there unconscious. The police took her to a hospital and it turned out she had alcohol poisoning. That was the event that was the turning point. It's when we lost control of her.

And then, her dad went away one weekend and she had a huge party at his house. She invited everyone she knew, even the US Navy came. They wrecked his house and robbed him of everything: carpets, cameras, jewelry. Her father lived in an exclusive neighborhood and he came home the next day to find bottles on the lawn and littered down the sidewalks. Caitlyn was so self-absorbed, she didn't care.

Halfway through grade 8, her dad told me that he couldn't handle her anymore. There were guys coming into the house at all hours or she would run away for days. One day he found these black men in the house with Caitlyn, who was only 13. They were kind of rough-looking and I think he said 1 of them had a knife.

Caitlyn came to live with me. Within days, she found the same crowd and she was just gone. I was worried all the time.

Our goal at that point was just to do anything to keep Caitlyn stable. We were terrified that she would overdose and die or that she would disappear. I was really worried about her going out onto the street. As a mother you really don't want to think your kid can trade sex, but I knew she was engaging in all kinds of sexual behaviors and guys would buy her clothes for sure. It's interesting that she thought trading sex was a form of being powerful because to me it's the ultimate in submission – selling your body.

I also talked to her about drugs and whenever I found them in her bag, I confiscated them and I never said a word. I figured she wasn't going to change, but she couldn't very well ask me for her marijuana or cigarettes. I would talk to her about drugs in general and I knew kids were experimenting, but I'd say, "You don't want to do it too much".

We didn't know what to do, but we thought that at least if she was in school and had a little routine, that it might keep her off the streets. Her school in Nanaimo wasn't keen on having her back. Her dad tried to get her into any private school, but no private school wants a kid in trouble, they want kids who make them look good.

We found an alternative school where all she had to do was show up. During this time, we went to psychologists and mediators and therapists. We thought maybe she was bi-polar because her behavior was so extreme and she was wasted all the time. I had to pick her up again from the hospital with alcohol poisoning. When I went to get her, I was just looking at this kid wondering what went wrong. She was skinny and white and had just about died. Why would she do this? She had everything. I just had no idea.

Her dad was hot and cold throughout. One moment, he would say that her behavior was completely outrageous and that he couldn't deal with her anymore and the next minute he would take her to Disneyland and buy her all these clothes. He was just in denial that his daughter could be on this path and he couldn't give her any meaningful boundaries for her behavior. After sending her away to live with me, he would change his mind and try to entice her back with gifts. I had no authority over her because he would always undermine the boundaries I tried to set.

In grade 9, she met a drug dealer/heroin addict, who was way older than her and I would have to go to his house to get her and she wouldn't want to leave. I would be driving there terrified of what I would find and terrified that I would have an accident.

It was around that time that my dad said, "You're going to kill yourself, Wanda. You have to let that kid go". I just cried. I failed this girl and I failed as a parent. A psychologist told me to put her in foster care, but her dad wouldn't let me. I have other friends who have lost their girls to the street. You try everything, but it's like she was a drowning person in a dangerous situation and my dad didn't want me to jump in and die too.

*What finally helped her?*

When Caitlyn was in grade 8, we tried to set up family mediation and we found a mediator that we thought was wonderful and we went quite a few times and tried to set up family mediation agreements. The mediator was very understanding, but she finally said, "Look, I can't do anything with this girl. She has no boundaries." She is the one who told me about Marion Roper. She said, "I know this woman who does cranial sacral therapy and it's really alternative, but it just might work for Caitlyn".

I started to take Caitlyn to Marion and that seemed to help her. As a scientist, the therapy really didn't make sense to me, but whatever, it worked. Caitlyn thinks it was her "tune ups" with Marion that helped her, but I think it was the whole combination of things we had been doing for so long.

**Yahoo.com**

The recent Craigslist posting for sex with a minor included nude photos of a 14-year-old "party girl". Recruited into prostitution by Justine Reisdorf, 19, and pimped out until Justine was arrested by the FBI for child sex trafficking.

Reisdorf's job as a front desk clerk at The Hampton Inn in Burnsville, Minnesota, gave her access to rooms. Since November of 2006, she had been pimping girls from 2 area high schools and used Craigslist and 'Live Links' to advertise the underage "party girls" charging 200 dollars for 1 girl and 375 for 3. She would text the girls at school with meeting times. This type of prostitution is hard to detect because it takes place at hotels, at parties and at people's homes through private arrangements.

Unlimited access to hard-core pornographic images, websites that facilitate "hookups" and chat rooms where sexual bartering takes place, shape teens' expectations and beliefs about what is normal sexual behavior.

10-year-old Beth, (name changed) sent Todd Peterson, 29, from St. Louis, Missouri, nude photos of herself after he befriended her over the Internet and mailed her a digital camera.

When Beth's mother learned what her young daughter had done, she e-mailed the man. Over the next 2 months, Beth's mother and Peterson communicated regularly and became romantically involved. She also allowed Peterson to continue chatting with Beth both online and by telephone. Peterson wanted to have sex with Beth, and her mother was preparing her to meet him at a San Diego hotel.

U.S. and Canadian authorities learned about Peterson's activities when he purchased a video containing child pornography from an undercover officer. The officers found explicit photos of Beth and other minors under the age of 12 on his computer following his arrest. While attempting to learn the identities of the children on Peterson's computer, they discovered Beth's mother's involvement.

On February 20, 2004, Peterson was sentenced to 13 years without parole. On April 9, 2004, Beth's mother was sentenced to 10 years in prison. Beth, now 13, lives with her grandparents. She recently got a small tattoo of a cat on her lower back. "My Nana didn't want me to get it because she said it's not ladylike, but it's just Miss Kitty. She's okay with it now."

I contacted Beth through her social worker. With Beth's family's permission, we began emailing. Beth has written about her mother's imprisonment, her parents' divorce, school life, and Peterson.

"It's disgusting to have your mom try to pimp you," she told me over the phone. "My Nan told me this summer how mom always wanted to get rid of me and put me up for adoption."

Beth writes because her grandparents are afraid to talk to her about what happened. "Even when my social worker visits, my Nan stays in the room."

Beth's social worker, Rose, says, "Her Nan feels so guilty. Their daughter did a horrible thing. Of course, shutting down when Beth needs to talk about her mother makes it seem like this little girl is responsible for what was done to her."

Beth's negative experience on the net has not scared her away from it or from meeting other people online. She posts on Nexopia, a teen dating site where people upload their photos and profiles, with information about their sexual orientation, height, weight, dating and living situation.

Scrolling through photos and profiles on Nexopia is fascinating and can eat up hours. The site offers a list of "hot girls" and "hot guys," or you can search by age, location, or gender.

If you are looking for 14-year-old boys anywhere in the world, you can limit your search to that criteria. Guys with usernames like "big-pimpin," "sexmachine," and "inspire," pose with their shirts off. Girls with usernames like "lover" and "lick-able" pout in their teeny bikinis.

You can scroll though photos of girls playfully flashing boob, butt, pink tongue and others pole dancing. Most teens will not call themselves "guccigurl," "fukc$luv" or "69lipz" to other teens, except online. Teens' use of sexual language is greater online than it is anywhere else. The net allows them to be outrageous and therefore desirable.

Our emphasis on sex, sex appeal and a worldwide obsession with brands have helped many girls shift from exploited to entrepreneur.[22] Girls are now setting the terms by which they will grant access to their bodies. They have started asking, "What's in it for me?" Girls are snatching the reins of their exploitation away from men in order to profit from it themselves.

Trading sex for money or gifts has never been easier. Log onto Yahoo!, enter the Schools and Education chat, scroll down the list of topics, and stop at the chat group titled "Teens Fuck For Cash" or "Baby and Pre-Teen Sex," or "Girls 13 & up for much older men," or "8-12 year-old girls for older men."[23]

Detective Randy Wickins, who heads Edmonton's Internet Exploitation Vice Unit, logs on, loads his stock photo of a demure-looking young girl, and waits. After a minute, he seems embarrassed that no one has "hit" on him. 30 seconds later, 2 guys are trying to chat with him. They ask his age. "13," he writes. One of them says, "I'm 29. Is that okay?"

He is then asked for his bra size. I offer my own, 34B. Whoa, suddenly 7 men are online trying to get his attention. One of them asks him if he shaves his pussy. Wickins writes, "Not likely!" Another asks how much for a cock ride. He says, "300". The guy says, "No problem" and asks, "Will I need a condom?" He is not deterred when Wickins writes, "Of course!"

The guy asks when they can meet. Wickins reminds him that he is in Maryland and "she" is in Edmonton. He says he can travel. Another man wants to know if "she" is willing to masturbate for him via webcam right now.

In the mid-1990s, Jennifer Ringley set up a webcam in her dorm room and subscribers paid her to watch. Known as the "Jennicam," it pioneered the "camgirl" explosion.

The predominance of online porn and the constant soliciting of sex

[22]"The global luxury goods business was up 27.7% in the U.S. and 56.2% in Hong Kong in the first five months of 2004." Betts, Kate. "Hey, Big Spenders." *Time*, 14 Sept, 2004. Ed.

[23]In 2005, Yahoo! Inc. said it will bar chat rooms that promote sex between minors and adults and restrict all chat rooms to users 18 and older. The social networking site MySpace faces 4 sexual assault lawsuits involving minors.

in chat groups have given girls a fast and easy way to make money without ever leaving their bedrooms. It is easy for a high school girl with access to a computer and webcam to exploit herself sexually, to see that behavior as brave and outrageous and to treat the money as sufficient incentive for any risk.

Camgirls direct their fans to online gift registry services such as Wishlist, Amazon, or Felicite.[24] The camgirl doing homework in her underwear asks, "Like what you see? Send me a gift." In the near future, Western Union and Paypal will dominate the camgirl industry. Girls are sliding into a form of prostitution without ever using the word.

"I looked into setting up a webcam, but I have a Mac and most of it is for PCs," explains Emma. Emma lives with her parents, a neurologist and a former ballerina, in Beverly Hills. "Also, the whole technical aspect of it was too much for me. I was in high school and I didn't have the time."

Emma responded to an ad in the back pages of *LA Weekly*. "It said $100 an hour for nude photography." "The guy came over to my house, I took off my clothes, and I started really digging it, like, big time. I was like, 'Wow, this is kind of hot. I've got some random dude in my room taking naked pictures of me and I'm looking all hot and shit and I'm getting paid for it.'"

Emma posed for 2 photographers. "To them, they were the ones in charge, but to me, I was getting what I wanted: a little thrill, a little bit of kink. I don't like to tease boys that I like, but paid teasing, knowing that someone wants you, then you're like, 'Yeah, I know, but tough,'" she says, laughing.

Emma's photos were arranged on a sample page and sent to webmasters. "They look at the pages, decide if they want to buy the package of 30 pictures, and then they charge people to look at those pictures on their site," Emma explains.

Within weeks, Emma's friend's brother found her on the Internet. "My friend called me up and was like, 'Were you on a porn site?' I was like, 'Oh, yeah.' She was like, 'My brother thinks you're hot.'"

Merlyn Horton, founder of the Safe Online Outreach Project cautions girls like Emma. "Online images live forever. If you're trading nude pictures of yourself for a CD player, you've sold out for millions of people viewing that image. It is an image that can come back and ruin your life".

Emma agrees. "I should have been paid more than $200. They're still making money off of my pictures. It's why I did escorting," she explains.

---

[24]Felicite suspended 100 accounts linked to camgirl sites following the 2002 murder of Christina Long, a 13-year-old girl, in Greenwich, Connecticut. Saul Dos Reis, a man she met online, strangled the 6th grader while they were having sex in his car at the Danbury Fair Mall.

# Emma, 18

It was the summer I was supposed to work for Human Rights Watch in Los Angeles; I had lined it up earlier during the school year, but then when I called them for my start date, they told me they didn't have anything for me to do, which was really disappointing.

I had also planned to spend part of the summer in Texas because I'm really interested in doing death penalty work. I spent the last year of high school writing to death row inmates in Texas. The one who wrote back is on death row for killing a police officer.

I figured after working with Human Rights Watch I would go down to Houston where the crime happened, visit the crime scene, read the court records and transcripts, visit him on death row. Maybe bring some attention to the case, if I could.

When my internship at Human Rights Watch fell through, my best friend invited me to go to Austin with her where she had found work. I found us a little apartment and my parents paid the first month's deposit. The day before we were supposed to leave, my friend told me that she had accepted a better job offer in Los Angeles and that she wouldn't be joining me.

My parents didn't care about the deposit and told me that I could just stay home for the summer and hang out, but the idea of hanging around the house living off of my parents sounded like a bummer. I didn't want to have a boring summer before starting at UCLA, so, I went by myself.

Before arriving in Austin, I thought I should have a fall back plan, in case, I couldn't find a job. So I researched the top escort agencies and I found an agency that seemed legitimate. I gave them a call and sent in my nude photos; they told me to call when I arrived.

One of the managers came over to the apartment the same afternoon I arrived and we had this long talk. He told me that all of their clients are regulars, some for decades, and that the agency has all of their personal information, including where they live, a social security number and work information. He told me they have a little pack of lawyers on staff, in case anything happened. He told me that if ever I felt uncomfortable, all I had to say was, "I'm sorry, something has come up." He told me to tell them that they would get a full refund.

I decided to give it a shot and see if I could do it even once.

The whole time before the date, I was just like, 'this is so hilarious. This is so typical of me. I'm in this city where I don't know anybody. I have no business being here and look at what I'm about to do.'

My first client was an outcall so I went to his house. He was really sweet. He knew that it was my first time ever. He let me play on his drum set, which was really cool, since I don't play the drums. He got me a glass of water and then we talked for a little while.

Before we did it, he was in the other room and I was in the bedroom and I was like, "oh my God, I'm actually going to do this." It wasn't a scary feeling. It felt more like that feeling you get before an adventure.

It was a really cool experience. I was treated kindly. In fact, I basically had my ass kissed—just worshipped—and I got paid $300 for the hour. The clients pay the agency separately.

In order for an escort agency to function under the law and not be considered a whorehouse, the understanding is that the men are paying the girls for the "pleasure of their company".

From a legal point of view, the $300 is for "hanging out" with the guy for an hour because you are not allowed to talk about the money or the sex. Even though the money is supposed to be for "hanging out", if you want to keep making money, you better have sex.

The men call themselves hobbyists. They have reviewing societies and a website where they write detailed reviews of the girls at different agencies. After my first review I got a lot of calls.

There are 2 kinds of calls. An outcall is where you go to the guy's place. For an in-call we used an apartment owned by the agency. All of the girls had a key to the place and we were expected to change the sheets and do the laundry after we were done. If we used the apartment, we gave the agency 15 bucks.

I was what they called a GFE, a girlfriend experience, which basically means that you act like you're the guy's girlfriend. When he arrives, you ask him how his day was and shoot the shit, which was great because I got to talk to them about their views on the death penalty.

The most lucrative dates are the 2–hour shows, which usually happened if the guy got a hotel room. I had a lot of married clients and if they were nervous about using the apartment, they got a room somewhere.

Most of my clients were from Dell Computers and I think most of them were married because I only ever saw them during the day, never at night. I also had a couple of doctors. Before I started working there, they asked me if there were any ethnicities I didn't want to have as clients. I don't care about color or race, but I was like—no criminal prosecutors and no cops—I don't want to sleep with people who are responsible for putting people on death row. Those people have just the most horrible jobs in the world and they really think they're helping people.

Escorting is the best job I've ever had. I like sex just as much as any guy. I think if the tables were turned and someone offered a guy 300 bucks to have sex, of course, they'd be down with it. They'd be like, "dream job". But the second a woman considers it, she obviously has problems, a bad childhood, whatever.

Somehow, a woman liking sex and God forbid getting paid for it is so anti-feminist, which is such bullshit. What I was doing was possibly the most politically subversive job I've had in my life.

*I ask her to elaborate.*

I was planting little seeds about how the death penalty is wrong. These middle-class, suburban Texans never heard anything like this before. Then I'd take my clothes off and they'd see the tattoo of a black fist just below my hip and they'd be like, "is that the black power symbol?" It's not, but it is my reminder to fight the good fight, to go for it.

Most of my clients were really decent guys. A few of the guys were fat or ugly and I had to tell myself, "oh honey, just keep your eyes closed and you'll get through it."

*I ask her why she had sex with the unattractive dates, when she was escorting for the adventure and not out of financial need.*

They were kind and gentle. One thing about Texans, they're gentlemen. They might have elected George W, but they're gentlemen. One guy gave me a full body massage, a glass of champagne, and fed me fresh fruit before anything even got started.

All of it was protected. If there was any pre-cum, I wouldn't suck dick. I would never let them cum in my mouth. There was this one guy who was a total germaphobe. He would not even touch my breasts without wearing gloves and then, he turns to me and asks me if I've ever heard of golden showers. I'm like, "that's when you pee on each other, right?" He was like, "would you be interested in that?" I was like, "Dude, I have no problem peeing on you, but you're just not going to pee on me." He was like, "No, no, I would never demean you in that way." He wanted me to pee on him. I was like, "okay, sure. When am I going to get to piss on some random dude again, right?"

There was only one guy who was a bit of jerk. I had let a couple of the guys do me up the ass because sometimes I really like it and when you're in the mood, you're in the mood. I'd just be like, "go for it". So this guy basically makes it pretty clear that for his hour, for the whole hour, he wants to do me up the butt. I don't mind a little bit, here and there, but for an hour?

I only worked as an escort for a month, but in that time I made over $10,000 and I didn't even work all the time. Basically, you call the dispatcher in the morning tell them the hours you want to work, if you want to work at all. I worked a few hours a day.

I saved almost all of my money, but I saw a lot of the girls blow their money on like 5 cars. Who needs 5 cars? Get a crappy car and use the money on rent and food and travel. Buy books. Go to school.

I met some of the girls during one of the social events set up by the agency. It's where a bunch of the regular clients and the girls meet at a restaurant for dinner. Most of the girls were either doing it full time or for the summer to help pay for college. Most of them were around my age.

My sister knows about this experience. All of my friends know. I don't talk about it with future employers, although I wish I could. I tried to get a job with Urban Outfitters and we were all in this group interview and they asked us about our people skills and I kind of wanted to say: I can meet anyone whether it's some guy that's going to pay me for sex or someone on death row and get along with them just fine. But no employer wants to hear that, so I don't bring it up.

## Metrotown Mall

In the parking lot of Dover Secondary School, 3 boys with long hair lean against a dented blue Taurus; the stereo cranks Ludacris.

A police cruiser is parked near the front entrance: Columbine and other high school shootings have made police presence a normal part of high school life.

A girl with straight, blonde hair, a perfectly powdered face, and lips touched with pink gloss glides by me. Dressed in a pink-shirt that barely reaches her midriff, she caresses her stomach absentmindedly. A blue jewel is nestled in her navel. Thin, clear bra straps have fallen from her shoulders; she does not seem to care. She has a boy on either side. One has his arm around her shoulders and the other has his hand on the small of her back, with a single finger looped in the thong that rides above worn, white jeans.

---

[25]McKeone, Marion. "FBI says that pimps are now flocking to the malls in search of young disease and drug free teens who they say can demand more money for sex," Sunday Tribune, 24 Aug. 2003 Pg 21.

In the office, there are 6 girls on the couch across from me. We are all waiting to see the school counselor. One has wet hair and her T–shirt is soaked. The female police officer looming over them later tells me that the tough-looking blonde doused the wet girl with a Snapple, calling her a "man-whore."

The counselor arrives and ushers me into his office. The girls stand in the doorway, yelling and complaining about each other. He escorts them to a conference room.

A young woman wanders into his office to use the phone. There is a small tattoo of a broken heart peeking from the sleeve of her T-shirt. She tells me about the girls and the ongoing battle over boyfriends.

"Most girls are labeled a slut, a bitch, or a loser," she says. "The drunk me always gets talked into messing around, which makes me a slut."

"Have you ever traded sex for anything?" I ask.

"Maybe drugs," she says.

The counselor returns and asks if she told me about the nude pictures. "A lot of girls use webcams to strip for guys," she says nonchalantly.

"We had a student who was dating a young man, and when they split up he put her naked photos on the Web. Everyone including her family saw them," he explains. Seeing the vice-principal, he runs out to speak with him. He returns a few minutes later with Samantha. She has pulled her long hair into a ponytail, and is wearing a sweat top. She looks more like a cute cheerleader than the sexy girl I had seen earlier in the hall.

Samantha, 16, had been recruited into prostitution at a mall.[25]

Seeing my recording gear, she says she is not prepared to talk about her experience at all. We chat for a few minutes about unrelated things and she asks me about the other girls I have interviewed. As I am leaving, she tells me to call her in the evening and scribbles her number on a sheet from the notebook she has been holding tightly against her chest.

I call Samantha's house that evening and speak with her mother who says she has encouraged her to tell her story. Samantha picks up the extension and tells me to meet her after school.

I am parked at the top of a long line of cars outside the school's front entrance. Samantha is easy to spot in the crowd. She is Jessica Simpson-pretty. She appears full of confidence in low-cut black jeans, sandals, and a sleeveless, green crop top. When she steps into the car, I see that her fingernails and toe-nails are French manicured and messy.

On the drive to a nearby mall, I her ask about the large, black bruise on her upper arm. She laughs and casually reveals that it was from a game of chicken with a boy. He punched her every time she lost.

She tells me that until last year, her family lived in San Diego. Her stepfather, who helped raise her from the age of 3, asked for a transfer to Nanaimo, to be close to his ailing mother.

She picks a Japanese restaurant and we are seated in one of the booths. The 4 men at the sushi bar periodically swivel to stare at her.

## Samantha, 16

My dad and I haven't had a good relationship since I was younger. I actually fight a lot with my parents.

When we moved to Nanaimo, me and Jasmine became instant friends at school, we were just so much alike. She comes from a very strict East Indian family. She has to do a lot behind her parents' back. It was similar to the situation that I had at home, with my curfew and not being allowed to drink. That's why we were pretty good friends too, we had the same situation, the same things, we both snuck out at night.

I really hated moving here and leaving my friends in San Diego, so I started skipping out of school, and my parents didn't like my new boyfriend, so I was sneaking out to see him and drinking, and I wanted to go out with my friends. Everybody was doing it, but somehow I was a bad person.

That's when Jasmine let me stay at her friend's place. Me and Jasmine wanted to party and I couldn't do that at home. I basically ran away and lived with her friend. He was a real gentleman. After a few weeks, he told me I had to leave because the police had come over to ask about me. I think my parents sent them, so I had no choice. I had to go home. I thought my parents would chill, but nothing changed. I couldn't see John, my boyfriend. I couldn't go out. I wasn't allowed to drink. Nothing.

*The nonchalance with which she describes moving in with a stranger is striking. She keeps talking as she pulls apart her dragon roll to eat the crunchy tempura bits.*

On Halloween, I was at John's place and I fell asleep there. I came home the next day but my parents were so mad, they told me I wasn't allowed to see him again. It was so unfair.

My dad started traveling again for work, so it was better at home because my mom's pretty easy and we're close. I felt like I was really trying at home. And then I asked if I could go to Vancouver, like, an hour away, with John's family. Without even talking to me about it, my mom just said no. They thought John was a bad influence. I decided to go anyway.

The morning John came to pick me up, it was snowing. I knew my mom was mad, so I went outside to tell him to wait at the bottom of the driveway. When I went back, my mom had locked the front door. I was standing outside in the freezing cold in my socks.

I just kept yelling, "Give me my fucking shoes," and she was telling me to fuck off. My mom threw my red high heels at me from her bedroom window and that's what I had to wear. It was a pretty big fight between me and my mom. We fight little fights, but not like this. I was swearing at her and she was swearing at me. It was pretty bad, because we're close, and when we do that we know it's something bad and it's hurting both of us.

*Samantha's house is perched on a hill with a long, curvy driveway. The surrounding houses have manicured lawns and SUVs out front.*

My dad was away at the time, but basically, they gave me an ultimatum. They said, "If you go, you're kicked out." I went, and when I came back I found my duffle bag outside, and so I had to live with my boyfriend. I got kicked out about a week before Christmas and my birthday, which is on the 26th, the day after Christmas. I spent Christmas with John's family instead of my own.

*One of the men at the sushi bar waves at her as he leaves. She seems flattered. Then, she is back to telling her story, as though she has told it a million times before.*

I was at my boyfriend's and I was doing anything I wanted. I was partying and I didn't have to respond to my parents. I was having such a good time, I didn't want to go back, but then my boyfriend wanted me to go home and work things out, so I called a few times, but I couldn't go back if things didn't change.

Eventually, my mom did tell me to come back and that basically I could do whatever I wanted, but by then I was really mad and I didn't want to go back. I had already been living at John's for 2 months. I was putting off going home, and then Jasmine told me she had a friend that we could stay with in Vancouver, and so we thought we'd go party one last time before I went home.

When my boyfriend found out, he told me not to go because he knows I'm naïve. He also knows that, together, me and Jasmine are not that smart. He said he didn't want me to go alone with Jasmine, but he couldn't come because he was working. He's pretty smart.

*The waitress brings Samantha a bowl of red bean ice cream.*

The first place we went in Vancouver was downtown. We were just walking around seeing what was going on. We just walked around and talked to people to see what was going on because we had nothing to do.

We phoned her friend when we got there, but her friend wasn't picking up so we had nowhere to stay, but we figured we would find somewhere to go when we were out partying. We weren't worried, we were just in the excitement of wanting to party and have fun.

We ended up getting some alcohol. We gave a guy 10 dollars and he bought it for us. After buying the alcohol we only had $10 each left because we had spent money getting there, buying food and buying alcohol. We had to save some money to get back home.

And then it started raining. It was raining pretty hard and we ended up walking for hours. We eventually took the Skytrain somewhere far from the downtown area and walked some more, and by then the trains and buses stopped running. It must have been 3 in the morning. We started to walk back on the highway to get back downtown, and a car picked us up. They drove us back downtown. I guess they felt sorry for 2 girls, in the rain, on the highway.

We got back downtown and started looking for somewhere to stay. It was 4 in the morning and we were tired, wet, cold, and we needed to sleep. A guy came by when we were asking for change for the pay phone to call Jasmine's friend again. He told us he was having a hotel party and that we could come. He gave us a couple quarters and he told us he was in Room 206 at the Best Western.

We phoned Jasmine's friend again and when he didn't pick up, we went to the hotel. They told us they were college guys. We drank with them and then we went to sleep. They were nice guys. In the morning we used their shower, got ready, and left.

We made our way to Metrotown Mall. We were just walking around. We didn't have any money and we were hungry, which is when we met 2 guys, Diddy and Ace. They were 2 black guys, who were very well dressed, and very handsome. They were going up an escalator and they made eye contact with us. We were sitting on a bench below, just flirting, smiling, trying to get their attention. They came back down the escalator and approached us.

Diddy was very polite. He asked us how we were, who we were with, where we were staying. They he asked us if we wanted to have lunch. They paid for our lunch. I should have known something was up when he pulled out a big wad of money just to pay for a small bill of Chinese food.

Then he started asking us a lot of questions. He asked us where we were from and why we were here. He wanted to know if we worked and if we had boyfriends. We told him we were older, because we didn't want them to think we were just 15. So we said we were 19.

I told him I had just been kicked out of my house and that I was living with friends, that I didn't have a place to live, and that I didn't know what I was going to do. I also didn't tell him that I had a boyfriend. They were really cute guys and we wanted to party, so I didn't want them to know about John.

They asked us if we wanted to party with them that night. Diddy gave us his cell number and told us to call them at 9:00. We just hung around the mall until that time and then we went back downtown.

We called him at 9:00 and he told us to call back at 9:30. We called him at 9:30 and he told us to start walking to this bar and that he would have a friend meet us and show us the way. His friend met us and took us to this place called the Mo Bar. You can barely see it because they turn off the lights so the police don't come by. When you step in it's light, but from the outside it looks like it's closed.

We got in there and everyone was about 25. They were all black. Mostly guys, but a few women. Me and Jasmine didn't know anybody, and Diddy still wasn't there. On the phone, Diddy had told us to talk to the DJ and he would hook us up with drinks, and he did.

I was approached by a lot of guys just party-talking, friendly-talking and Jasmine ended up getting very angry with me. She was already drunk and so was I, and after awhile she left. I think she was angry because more guys approached me and she was feeling left out. She ended up storming out and leaving me with our stuff, which was just one small bag. I thought she was going to come back eventually, but she didn't.

Half an hour later, everyone was leaving the party and Diddy still hadn't shown up, so I left with Shaun and Rex, these 2 other guys I met there. They asked me if I needed somewhere to stay and said that I could stay with them, so I did. I went to Shaun's house that night and I slept there.

In the morning, we went back to the mall, where I first met (Shaun's) friend. My clothes were all dirty because I'd worn them for 2 days straight. He picked out some clothes. He bought me a tank top, tight, tight jeans, and a white, furry jacket. It looked very expensive, high-class, like glamorous. To me it was just a nice gesture. He was just being a really nice guy because my clothes were dirty and I couldn't wear them again. I figured it was just a nice gesture.

On the way home, Shaun started bringing up the subject of money: how to make a lot of money, how he has a lot of money for everything he needs, and how he can support me and give me a place to live. He knew about my living situation and how I had been kicked out and now my friend had left me, so I didn't really have anyone and I didn't have anyone supporting me. He took the opportunity to gain my trust and tell me that he could support me, give me a place to live, and that he could have everything for me, everything I ever needed, and the party life.

It obviously sounded great.

I was hearing all these great things: a lot of money and new clothes and having a place to live, which I didn't have at the time. To me he seemed like a friend, a confidant, someone I could trust, who would be loyal to me. He said that if I was loyal to him, he would be loyal to me. He gained a lot of my trust through that.

He waited until we got back to his house before talking about prostitution. He told me that it would only take me 2 nights to work off the clothes he had bought me.

I was shocked. I hadn't asked for clothes, but I basically had taken the clothes without knowing the terms. Now I knew what he was getting at, and although it wouldn't ever cross my mind to go do something like that, when it was put in front of me I felt like I had to do it.

I already felt like I was obligated to pay off my clothes, because that's the first thing he said: "It'll only take you 2 nights to work it off." So, at that point, I didn't argue. I didn't argue with anything he said. I didn't really say much. He did all the talking. I did the nodding. I occasionally said "Okay" or "Yes."

I wasn't protesting at all. I was going to do it. It was just going through my head that I was going to do it. I was listening to everything he was saying and thinking about how I was going to do it.

He told me how to work the streets. He said that I should turn and walk the other way if a cop was coming. He told me the price range, and what to ask for each trick. He told me that the first question to ask when I approached a car is, "Are you a cop?" He told me, if it's a cop, he has to tell you, even if he's undercover. Then he told me to ask the person if they want a date. You should only get in the car if the person wants a date, and that's when you negotiate your price for whatever they want.

I think I was curious a little bit that maybe this would work, because having a place to live, having a lot of money sounded like a good deal. So that night I did go to work.

He told me when to get dressed and to wear more makeup than normal. I wore the jeans he had bought me that day, the tank top, and the jacket. I had my high heels with me. I wore my hair up. It felt weird getting ready. Usually when you get ready to go out, you want to look nice for people. Now, I was getting ready to go out on the streets. I don't know how to explain it. I wasn't really thinking, "Oh, I'm getting ready to go be a prostitute," I was thinking, "I've just got to look really, sort of, slutty," and that's what I was doing.

When I was ready, he checked me over. Then he drove me downtown to Franklin Street in Vancouver where the younger girls work. He gave me condoms and he told me to keep a pack of condoms with me at all times. He also gave me a phone card so I could call him at 3 or 4 in the morning when he would pick me up. He dropped me off at 10:30 p.m.

The first time I did it, it was pretty weird. Negotiating the price was probably the most awkward part, probably even more awkward than doing the trick. I would say, "I need $100 for this," and they'd say, "Well, I'll give you $80 because you're pretty." Almost all of the guys would ask me not to use a condom. They offered more money if I did it without one.

A lot of the men were in their 40s. There were a lot of Asian guys. Around midnight, richer businessmen came out. Later than that, younger guys with less money, probably drunk from the bars, came looking for a lay or a blowjob.

When I was actually doing the trick, my body was there but my mind was somewhere else. If anything was running through my mind it was just to get done. I was waiting for it to be over to get my next trick to get my money.

Once I negotiated the price, I didn't feel I could refuse anything they wanted. Once you're in their car, going to their location, they're in control. You can only set limitations when you first talk. I told them I wouldn't do anything anal and I wouldn't kiss on the lips. A lot of men want to be kissed because that's what turns them on. I tried to avoid it when I could, rather than saying no outright.

I did have one odd guy approach me. I got in his car. He didn't want to be around because the cops were in the area, so we went over a bridge to a park somewhere. He didn't want to meet my prices after we'd already negotiated, and at this point I didn't know where I was. I didn't know what price to negotiate. He only had $50. I couldn't go that low for a lay, I just couldn't. I had to meet certain requirements. So, he just had me take off my clothes and he gave himself a hand job. I got my $50 and that was probably the weirdest one I had out of them all.

The richer, older men took me to their apartments. The younger men took me to a nearby park and we did it in the car. There was also a rundown neighborhood close by and they would parallel park and the house lights would be out because it was so late and we'd do it right there in front of people's houses.

At the end of the first night I had $160. I called Shaun around 3 and he came to pick me up. At 3, the traffic stops; nobody comes looking for anything anymore. He took all of the money and searched my purse to make sure I wasn't hiding anything, and to make sure I didn't have any extra, and just to see what I had with me at all times. The money didn't meet his requirements. He said it was okay but that I would do better the next night.

The next day, I woke up pretty late and we made our way to a Laundromat, and honestly I couldn't tell you much more about that day, except that Shaun wanted me to call my mom because she had been calling him. I guess when Jasmine came back alone, my mom and my boyfriend got worried. Jasmine told my mom that I left her at the club and that she didn't know where I was. My mom sent the cops to her house to talk to her, which is when she gave my mom Diddy's cell number. My mom started calling Diddy, and then the police started calling him. Diddy called Shaun and Shaun told him not to tell them anything. Eventually Diddy gave Shaun's number to the police.

The police started calling Shaun's cell, but he wouldn't pick up. Then my mom called and left a message on his cell, and that's when he took me to a pay phone and told me exactly what to say to her. He told me to tell my mom that I was living with a friend named Peter, that I had a job, that I was okay, and to tell the police to stop calling. So I did. She told me she would tell the police to stop calling, which is what I told him.

*The waitress brings the check. We decide to finish the interview in the car when a family of 4 is seated at the next table. As we cross the street to the parking lot, an old man in a white pickup whistles at Samantha. She rolls her eyes. It is strange to be with someone who commands so much attention.*

We finished the laundry and then we made our way to his friend's house. I was the only white female in a room full of black men. They were playing dominoes, drinking, eating dinner. They didn't communicate with me. There was no interaction between us except they would look at my body or watch what I was doing.

They knew that Shaun was a pimp and that they couldn't talk to me. They weren't allowed to talk to me. I didn't feel comfortable at all. Even Shaun didn't talk to me until 9, when he pulled me aside to get ready. I got ready in their bathroom and he took me downtown.

That night, I got picked up by a younger, white male. He took me to his apartment; he wanted an hour of my time for $80, which was fine because he wanted to talk to me first. A lot of people want to make a connection with you. You have to pretend you're involved in what they're saying and show some sympathy. Once they're comfortable then they want what they're asking for.

This guy got comfortable enough for me to give him what he wanted, but then he didn't want to drive me back. This was already after an hour and I only had $80 to show for it. I knew I needed to make a lot more money to satisfy Shaun.

At this point, I was nervous. I didn't know where I was and didn't have a license plate. He eventually took me back at 1 in the morning. He didn't have more money to give me, so he gave me weed, which he told me I could give to Shaun.

When I got back, I went to the 7-Eleven and called Shaun. He hung up on me when I told him I only had $80. I walked back to the street to make a little more money. Eventually I got 1 more trick for $60. Shaun picked me up at 4 and took me back to the house, where he took the money.

I was nervous about not making enough money for him, but he told me that I would do better the next night. He was very controlling. I felt as though he was above me, so when he told me to do stuff I felt obligated to do it.

He told me that the police were still calling him, and that my uncle had called and left a threatening message. At this point my parents didn't know that I was being prostituted. Shaun wanted the police off his back, so he told me that I should go home on Saturday and talk to my mom. He wanted her to see that I was okay. He told me to tell her that I was moving to Vancouver, and he told me to bring my stuff back with me on Sunday, when he would meet me. He said we would go to Las Vegas when I got back. I was motivated the next night to make enough money to please him.

The next night, I went to the streets and he went clubbing. I had about 6 tricks that night and I made $400. He was happy about the money and he and his friends came and picked me up at 3. I rode in the first car with his friend and his father. Shaun was in the car behind us with another guy.

We drove for awhile and then pulled over, at which point Shaun came up to the car and I gave him the money. We did the "How much money?"

"How many tricks?" Then, he leaned over and told me, as I was sitting next to his dad, that his dad wanted a little something. I couldn't argue because it was his father. He told his father that I would give him something and that I would do it while we were driving to the next house. He told me to give his father a blowjob. He got back in the other car. His friend drove as I gave his father a blowjob.

We made another stop at a house and I assumed I was done for the night. Shaun approached me and told me that his other friend had paid for me for the night. He told me that he would pick me up in the morning to take me home. This was the first time I felt really angry.

I had no choice. I went with his friend, who picked up some food for me. I ate food, then I had a shower. I was in his bed with him to have sex with him, but I was so tired. It was about 5 or 6 in the morning and I had done so many tricks already. He wanted a lay, but when he started it hurt a lot. I was very dry. It was almost like rape because it hurt so much, and he kept telling me that it was okay. He didn't have a condom and I didn't have any left because I had used mine already.

He talked me into it by saying, "It's okay. I've already paid for you." I was obligated to do it. It still hurt. It hurt a lot. He took lotion and lubricated himself thinking it would help. Afterwards, I went upstairs to the bathroom. When I came back down, he had passed out. I went to sleep on the couch.

In the morning, Shaun came to get me. I got dressed and they took me to where I could catch the ferry home. He gave me $20 to pay for the ticket and to get something to eat. On the ferry ride home, I knew that I wasn't going back.

*There is not a single moment during which Samantha shows any emotion while telling her story. She does not cry; her voice is steady and clear. These events took place less than 2 months ago. She is numb.*

When I got back to Nanaimo, I went to Jasmine's house and told her the story, and that's when she took me to see our school counselor. He took me home and I was reunited with my mom. She knew something terrible had happened, but she didn't know the whole story until I gave my statement to the police and she read it herself. It was too hard to tell her to her face because we're so close and I knew that it would hurt her a lot.

The police told my mom they were investigating Diddy and Shaun for pimping some other girls, but I don't think they ever made any arrests. The officer who talked to my mom told her that I wanted to do this because

I wanted to hang out with gangsters. I think that's kind of harsh, because she was pretty nice to my face and then she made it sound like it was my fault. It just sounded good at the time, but it's not like I ever thought, "I want to be a prostitute."

*I turn off my tape recorder and Samantha rolls down her window. She tells me that she has not been feeling well and that she needs to make an appointment to see her doctor. She pulls a spiral book from her bag and makes a note for herself. On the drive to her home, she is sad.*

How could something like this have happened to me? You never think it will happen to you, but it happened so easily, and it really can happen, seriously, to anyone, just under certain circumstances.

Six weeks have passed since I interviewed Samantha. She emails me about her boyfriend, but when I call to speak with her, she tells me that her mother needs someone to talk to and passes the phone to her.

Lynne is a stay-at-home mom with 2 young children, she is funny, warm and looks like a young Jane Fonda. If I call at night, she takes the phone into the garage of her 3-story house, the only private place she can find. During the day, when everyone is out, she will take her cigarettes and a cup of tea and head into their fenced backyard. I hear the screen door creak as she walks in and out of the sunshine.

We talk about relationships and her past. She tells me she is sick of pretending to friends that her family is not falling apart. We talk about Samantha.

## Lynne, Samantha's mom

Here's something I bet she didn't tell you: when she was 13, she fucked 2 guys in the back of a car. I thought that was really bizarre since Sam didn't really even care about these 2 guys. You expect your daughter to have sex, but not with 2 black guys in the back of a car, after school, in broad daylight, in a cul de sac in your own neighborhood.

*She takes a long drag of her cigarette.*

I learned about my daughter's activities from a neighbor who called to tell me to keep Samantha away from their daughter. The whole school was talking about it: a note had been passed around describing it. I confronted

Sam that evening. She admitted it readily and had a cry. We talked a bit, but Sam says what she thinks you want to hear to get you out of her face. She said, "Yeah, I know I made a mistake. I'm not going to do that again."

Sam also said it was the first time she'd had sex, but I don't believe her, because it seems to me to go to that length, you have to be pretty far along sexually.

These 2 guys were black, which to me wasn't an issue at all except her boyfriend is black and then the guys who were prostituting her were black. I think she has an unhealthy obsession with black men. I really haven't analyzed it because I don't want it to be a race issue.

I hate to say it, but Sam and I are a lot alike. She chooses bad people, and when we moved here from San Diego, she was into John, her boyfriend, and only John, and that's sort of where the real problems started.

When we first moved here we lived with my in-laws. John came to pick her up and her grandfather told him to take good care of her and to bring her home on time. Well, Samantha didn't come home that night. At 2:30 in the morning she still hadn't come home. She had left John's number, and I just kept calling her there, but they ignored the phone. When she came home the next day, she didn't explain it beyond saying she had fallen asleep.

I was totally embarrassed in front of my in-laws, and James, my husband, who has been her stepfather since the time she was 3, was livid. James forbade Samantha from seeing John again. I stuck up for Samantha's boyfriend because I thought that was too harsh given that it was one incident, so I told her she could see him. My daughter was really upset. It wasn't just about sticking up for him. I didn't want to see her so upset and I didn't want her sneaking around.

When I look back at all the times in San Diego when I didn't back up my husband, I thought he was an asshole, but I think he was right and not that different from what other parents do. I guess I didn't see that he should have been mad when she didn't come home by curfew or when she snuck out. It's just that I'm a pushover.

After that first time when Samantha didn't come home, I thought she had learned her lesson, but things deteriorated. I'm sure that moving to Nanaimo made things worse for her, but it's not like she was a little angel in San Diego. The one thing I do know is that she didn't get caught all the time. Now she doesn't care what people think. She doesn't care who sees her drunk or stoned. Now she doesn't have enough self-respect to hide it.

When she hooked up with John and then Jasmine, she became a different person. She started with late nights, not calling, getting drunk, stoned, skipping out of school, sneaking out.

She and Jasmine would go to teen night at the pool and then get picked up by random guys.

The first time she came home drunk I grounded her for a month. I also talked to her school counselor and the vice-principal at her school, because she had complained to them about being grounded. They told me that the grounding was unfair, that all kids party and that all I need to know is where she is, and that I have to accept that as being okay.

I will never let people push me around like that again, but at the time, I was influenced by what they said and so we let her off. Now that I think of it, for the vice-principal to be telling me that I'm doing something wrong for grounding her because she came home drunk is absurd.

I don't know what happened to Sam to make her into such a difficult person, but I think some of it is because of her stepdad. When we lived in San Diego he was rarely at home. He has probably spent more than half of our marriage traveling, so I've been like a single mom. Now he's home every evening and he's strict. I hate the way he deals with the kids, but if I go back and look at it, I see there's nothing wrong with saying, "No, you can't stay out until 1." It's the way he says it, though. It's the sarcasm. He doesn't show them that he's listening to them. He's the kind of dad who lectures.

At this point, Samantha was still allowed to see John, which was my doing, and on Halloween she came and she talked to us about staying out until midnight because it was a school night. I thought that was really fair and James thought she was really being respectful by asking our permission, but then she just didn't come home. Of course, James was furious because he felt she violated his trust. When she did finally come home, he told her she was forbidden from seeing John.

This was the next phase of even bigger problems for us: she started running away. The police had to bring her back once but they told me that they couldn't make her come home.

At 14, if she chooses to sleep at a 40-year-old guy's house, I have no right to take her out of his house if she doesn't want to leave. Once when she ran away I knew she was at her boyfriend's, and then I didn't know where she was the other 2 times.

We were going through this stuff twice a week. It was constant. There was always crap going on. Everything was bad. She came and went as she pleased. She wouldn't lift a finger around the house. She never helped with her siblings. She would not so much as put her own plates in the dishwasher. Then, in the middle of all of this, she asks if she can go away with John to

Vancouver. I thought she was out of her mind and I told her as much.

It didn't make any difference to her because that night she was preparing to go. She said, "I'm going. I don't care what you say." I do remember that was the first time I said, "Fuck you, Samantha." I was so fed up, I probably said something like, "I hope you do fucking go, I'm just sick of you."

In the morning, she was getting ready and I was shaking. I was so mad. I could not believe she was actually going to go. It wasn't even that it was a trip to Vancouver; it was that she could be so defiant. It was also that she was going away to spend time with her boyfriend's family when there was so much crap going on in our family.

On many nights I had to call the hospital and the police to find out where she was. It was no coincidence that her plans coincided with one of James's business trips. He did talk to her on the phone in the morning, which made no difference. We decided to give her an ultimatum. We told her that her duffle bag would be outside if she went.

I paid for that mistake.

Today I realize that I did kick her out. At the time, I chose to look at it like she left. When she was getting ready in the morning, I told her that if she leaves she will find her bag outside.

When her boyfriend and his mom pulled up to our house, Samantha ran out in the snow without shoes or a jacket, which is when I locked the door on her. I was absolutely crazed. We were swearing at each other through the door. She was yelling, "Give me my fucking shoes," and I was yelling, "No. You're not getting anything from this fucking house."

Then I threw her red high heels at her. I thought they matched her outfit. I took them and went around the back and threw them so they practically hit the car. She grabbed them and literally ran for the car.

Then I packed her bag. I was so furious. I looked in her purse before I packed it and she had obviously prepared to spend the night somewhere because she had a change of underclothes and a change of jewelry.

She called me that night when she got back and asked me what I wanted her to do. I told her that her bag was on the porch.

I thought it would pass. In my heart I thought that a couple days would pass, we would talk and it would pass. But she didn't call and I didn't call her. Then she called and said, "Are things going to change around here?" I told her, "The deal here is that if you're going to live here, the rules are basic: come home at night, go to school, let us know where you are, and be respectful to your sister and brother." That phone call ended pretty fast. I don't know what she was expecting.

She called again and said, "What are you guys going to do differently?" She had a nasty, cold attitude. She was calling me, telling me that we had to change for her to come home. Eight weeks after Samantha left, I gave in. My heart was broken. I just wanted her to come home.

She called on New Year's Eve. She was sad. Her boyfriend had gone out without her. Things had gotten rough at John's place. His mom wanted her to leave. She told me she would call me the next day so I could come pick her up, but she didn't call.

A day later, her boyfriend left me a message saying it was urgent that I contact him. He told me that he wanted me to stop Samantha from going away with Jasmine. He said he was worried that they would end up at a club in downtown Vancouver, meet some guys, sleep with them, and maybe get into trouble.

Before she went away with Jasmine, John and his mom had told her they wanted her to go home. You need to understand her state of mind. She probably felt kicked out from his house, too. John's mom was upset because Samantha had been entertaining other boys in their home when John wasn't there.

There was nothing I could do. There was no way I could reach her. John said Jasmine knew some people in Vancouver, so I thought they'd go party and then they'd come home. But Jasmine returned home without Samantha. John called me to tell me Jasmine was back and Samantha wasn't.

I filed a missing person's report the next day. Jasmine didn't tell me much at all. She told me that they got into a fight and that Samantha walked away, but I don't believe that because Samantha had all their stuff. I called the police and they went and talked to Jasmine and John. Jasmine gave me a man's cell number a day or so after that, but Jasmine still hadn't mentioned anything about prostitution at this point.

I called the cell number and asked the man who answered if he knew Samantha's whereabouts. I told him to tell her that there was a missing person's report on her. I also told him that I would be giving the police his number since he was the last person to see her alive.

I gave the police, my brother, and her school counselor this man's cell number. My brother called him a few times. I don't know how he did it, but he scared this man into giving us Shaun's cell number.

Samantha called me from a pay phone soon after. I remember the feeling of listening to her robotic voice. It was so creepy. She said, "I'm in Vancouver. I'm with a friend. I'm fine. Don't worry. You can tell the police to stop calling. I gotta get off the phone, someone needs to make a 911 call." I didn't realize that she was in trouble. I thought she was just so angry that she was unemotional.

I was obliged to call the police to tell them that Samantha was okay. The officer told me that the cell number belonged to a guy who was known to police and that he was part of an ongoing investigation. They didn't tell me anything else.

After Samantha called, I called Jasmine and John, and that's when Jasmine told me there was a guy at the club who was talking to Samantha about prostitution. She said they asked her if she knew how much money she could make as a prostitute. Jasmine said that Samantha seemed interested and that's why they fought. I called the police right away with this information, but there was no one I could talk to. The officer in charge of her file was off duty.

I called my brother and the school counselor. There was nothing we could do; it was really just a waiting game. Truthfully, I never believed that she could be a prostitute. Even when the word came up, I honestly never thought that it could happen to her.

Samantha called me again the next night to ask me to tell the police to stop calling. She told me she couldn't talk, but that she was coming home. A few days after that she did come back, but she went to Jasmine's place first. Jasmine took her to the school where she talked to the counselor, and then he called and told me he had my daughter and that he was bringing her home.

I was watching for her and I ran outside when I saw her counselor's car. I remember her walking up the driveway; she was wearing this furry jacket. I remember thinking, "God, that looks like a pimp jacket." She dresses hoochie anyway, but she also had on a new shirt, tight jeans, and high heels. It was surreal to see her this way. She wasn't able to look at me, and at this point I didn't know everything that had happened to her, but I didn't care. She looked like she was ready to bolt, like she was going to leave again. I told her I loved her and that I was glad she was home. I asked her to stay.

I think it might have been the police report and reading her statement that made it real for me. The rest came slowly. I'm still learning parts of it. She wasn't scared to tell me, but she couldn't get into any detail about it.

Frankly, I didn't think I could talk to her about it anyway. I talked to a female officer for about 2 hours after reading her statement. Her take on Samantha was that she is a party girl.

Samantha explained it by saying she felt she had nowhere else to go and thought these guys were going to look after her. She felt as though everyone had turned against her: Jasmine, John, John's mom, her own family. I can see her desperation. She just accepted that this was her destiny and that this was her job now and that this was how she would survive in the world. I don't know what they did or said to her. I don't think she clearly understood the gravity of the situation.

In retrospect, I think John, her boyfriend, genuinely cared about Samantha. He tried to convince her to return home each time she ran away. He was right to be suspicious of Jasmine's motives. I also believe Jasmine knowingly delivered Samantha into the lion's den. I don't know if she got anything out of it, but I think she saw that Samantha was vulnerable and she helped create the circumstances for this to have happened.

It's not that hard for a girl to be talked into something given the circumstances. I remember being persuaded into things that I knew were wrong, but I couldn't say no. Maybe because sex is no big deal today, girls are able to take it one step further and treat prostitution as just one more thing to try out. Every girl's Cinderella story is to be rescued like Julia Roberts was in *Pretty Woman*.

After Samantha returned home she had herself tested for pregnancy and disease. She told me that everything was negative, including the pregnancy test, which could have been a false negative.

She had an abortion on Monday and we picked her up from the drunk tank on Friday. I don't think that she's really dealt with any of it and she refuses to see anyone. She may not even know how this experience has affected her.

I tried to take her to see a counselor, but when we got there she wouldn't get out of the car. She told me that she only agreed to the appointment because she wanted me to get therapy. She's definitely unhappy and I don't know how to help her.

# A High School Prostitution Ring

"I was recruited by a girl at school who pretended to be my friend. She always had money. She was always going to parties and she was always all bouncy and happy," explains Lauren, 15.

Lauren was part of the largest teen prostitution ring in Edmonton's history, involving over 50 school girls, between the ages of 12 and 16.

"She was coming home with hundreds of dollars every night, new clothes, new piercings, so I called the police," Angie, Lauren's mother, explains.

Detective Randy Wickins of the Edmonton Vice Unit followed Lauren to 3 different houses over a 2-week period where she met men for sex. Her cell phone records showed 2 numbers of known pimps.

Three weeks later, Wickins and a team of investigators arrested 5 men, ranging in age from 34 to 50, for having sex with persons less than 18 years of age.[26]

I interviewed 3 of the girls who had pressed charges, 2 weeks after the

---

[26]Williams, Ian. "Pockets of cash lead police to teenage prostitution ring: Noticing daughters had too much money at Christmas, Edmonton mothers alerted police," Vancouver Sun, 27 Feb. 2003.

case closed.

Lauren now lives with her aunt in a new, suburban development just outside of the city of Edmonton. There is a Church of Scientology nearby and the high school she attends is within walking distance.

Lauren's aunt, who has scraggly blond hair and red, wind-burnt cheeks, asks me to interview Lauren in the computer room where there is also a large aquarium full of colorful fish, a dusty treadmill and stacks of women's magazines.

Lauren's hair hangs in 2 messy braids held with mismatched clips. She is dressed in sweats and one of her boyfriend's checkered shirts. Her voice is soft and babyish and she giggles a lot.

## Lauren, 15

When I first started grade 8, I tried to wear heels because all the other girls were wearing them, but I'm already tall, so it just made me feel like a giant. I discovered Fubu sneakers, which you can dance in.

Looks are not that important to me, but people say I'm pretty. I have bushy eyebrows and long hair, which I mostly wear in a ponytail. I don't wear a lot of makeup and I dress in T-shirts and jeans. Sometimes, I wear eye shadow, but that's it.

*Lauren gets up to peer at the fish. She opens a small container and scatters some of the flakes into the tank. She drops back onto the chair, pulling her knees up under her.*

In grade 8, I went to class regularly and I had a lot of friends. I was an honors student with English as my best subject. I was in the school band and I raised money by selling chocolates to go on a band trip. I volunteered a lot of time to the Kiwanis Builders Club where I raised money through basketball tournaments for different groups.

I was also cheerleader, but I hated doing the whole "smiley, clappy" thing, so I quit after a while. It felt too much like a cult. I was a Jehovah's Witness until I was 10, but I didn't believe in God until last year. Now I pray regularly.

My favorite food is Hawaiian pizza and Coke, which I used to buy on Fridays when I got my allowance. I have a younger sister who I share my allowance with because she likes to hoard hers and look at it. I like to spend money. I used to baby sit every week to make extra money.

Most days after school, I would spend a lot of time in my room on my purple inflatable chair reading *Cosmo* or Stephen King books. I read *Carrie* in a day. My room is messy all the time. I even do my own laundry, but there are still clothes on the floor all the time. I have a huge canopy bed. My mom just got me a TV and DVD player. I have a black light that shines purple, which makes white things glow. I still have my lava lamp from when I was a kid.

In grade 8, my walls were covered with pictures of rappers, even ones I didn't know. I tried really hard to be into rap, even though I didn't care about it. I was really into *Powerpuff Girls*, but they're a bit embarrassing.

I still sleep at my granny's on most weekends to keep her company. We're super close. I can tell her anything. She's a good listener and everything she says makes sense; everything she tells me to do works.

When I went out, I didn't really have a curfew, but I was expected to be home by 9 on school nights and by 11 on weekends. On the weekends, me and my friends spent a lot of time at the mall. We would go dancing at GalaxyLand or play video games.

When I was 13, I would try to dance like the girls in music videos; me and my friend Leyla practiced Mariah Carey moves in my room. I thought that if I danced like the girls in the videos guys would like me.

I also spent a lot of time wondering if boys liked me. I would go to blunttruth.com and send anonymous surveys to friends to find out what they thought about me. I spent a lot of time chatting on MSN and surfing music and clothing sites.

My mom and I have a funny relationship because we fight all the time. We never stay mad at each other, but we bicker a lot. My mom says that I'm like her and that I seem to have to learn everything the hard way.

She works in a hospital emergency room, so she's stressed a lot. Before I moved in with my aunt, the nights she worked late, I would wait for her and she would always come home with a green Aero bar for me. We'd watch TV and hang out. My favorite shows are *Days of Our Lives* and *The Simpsons*. Sometimes I would tape *The Simpsons* for her and we'd watch it together; it was nice. *The Lost Boys* is my favorite movie.

I wasn't a total goody-2-shoes, but I was getting good grades and going to parties and drinking, so it was, like, normal. I've never done a lot of drugs, but I do speed sometimes when I'm bored and my drink of choice is beer.

Everything in my life changed when I turned 14, which is also when I lost my virginity. It was planned, but it was horrible. I was kind of joking that I wanted to lose my virginity, but then this guy I liked was serious, so I did it. It was definitely one of the most boring experiences of my life.

*Laughing she tells me that she was not sure if they had done it, since it was not at all "the way it is supposed to happen." Her face turns dark and unhappy. She twists one of her braids and tells me that she became depressed afterwards when she realized that they really had had sex.*

After that, everyone started calling me a slut. The whole school year was a struggle. The boys were constantly harassing me at my school. At the end of that year, my marks dropped and I hated school. My mom was also dating this freak, so we were always fighting about that, too.

*She excuses herself and returns with cookies and 2 glasses of purple juice.*

That summer was okay, but I was looking forward to high school. I was hoping to find some new friends. I didn't want to hang out with girls who were only interested in partying. I really thought of myself as a good girl and a girly girl.

I am very giggly, my favorite color is pink, I have fake nails, and I just got a pink backpack. It's a *SpongeBob SquarePants* back-pack. *SpongeBob* lives in a pineapple under the sea. He goes jelly fishing. *SpongeBob* replaced *Hello Kitty* in my life.

I'm not shy, but it's hard for me to make friends right away, so I was lonely. At school, Monika was always friendly to me and she invited me to party at Carlos's house. Carlos is Spanish, 21, and hot.

*She gets a dreamy look in her eyes and squeals when I ask her if she was in love with Carlos.*

Monika would say, "You're pretty, you should come." I didn't go, until Denise came along. Denise was dating my friend Cameron, but she also spent a lot of time at Carlos's place. She invited me to hang out at Carlos's apartment and to meet his hot Spanish friends. I went, one day, mostly because I was bored.

There were usually 4 or 5 guys there, including Carlos, his cousins, his brother, and some friends. You looked pretty when you went to Carlos's place. We did shots of tequila with them, got drunk, and had sex. It was fun. They would say, "Come to the room," pick one of us, and we would go. You didn't have to have sex with them, but if you didn't they were like, "Whatever, you're a skank anyway."

Carlos was very good looking and so were his cousins and friends. Denise liked Carlos, so he told her, "If you sleep with all of my friends, I'll sleep with you." So she did. We all did, but after awhile Carlos and I started dating.

Carlos moved from his apartment to a house after we hooked up. He needed more room for his 4 cars. One was a Cadillac; I'm a Cadillac girl. He told me he does construction, but I don't think you make that much money in construction.

Actually, I saw him sell coke. We would be in his bedroom at 3 in the morning and someone would come to his door and he would come back with 4 grand. There was money everywhere.

When we were going out, I only saw him very late at night. He would call my house after midnight and tell me to come over. Sometimes my mom would pick up the phone and yell at me, but she couldn't do anything because I would tell her that if I couldn't see him I would run away. There was nothing she could do; I would call a cab and go.

There were a lot of things that happened that led me into prostitution. My mom's relationship with her freakish boyfriend became really serious and she began spending all of her time with him. She spent more time with him than she did with me and my sister. I was really angry because I felt like she forgot about us.

I also become better friends with Denise, and Denise always had money.

One day, Denise and I were at my computer downloading music illegally because we were bored, and she asked me, "Do you want to know how I make my money?" I said, "Sure. How do you make your money?" She told me that she sleeps with Asians. She told me that, in 2 minutes, she makes 60 bucks.

Now that I think about it, we weren't charging enough.

When she told me about it, I didn't say anything to her. I just thought it was something I could do because she said it only takes 2 minutes. She said it would be over before I knew it and it was only sex and I wanted money. I wanted to go shopping and I didn't want to have a job. If I could make all that money in 20 minutes, 2 hours ... why not?

A few weeks after that she asked me what I thought about what she was doing. I told her that I thought it was all right and not such a terrible thing to do. She didn't ask me outright if I wanted to do it, but she was trying to see if I would do it. Then, she called me a few nights later. It was 8 at night and I was napping because I was going dancing later.

She told me to get dressed so that we could to go to a club called 4Play, which is owned by a fat guy who lets in underage kids. She came to my house to pick me up and told me that we would be meeting some friends in front of a store. We started walking and a really ugly green [Toyota] RAV4 with 2 guys in it pulled up next to us. Luu Dang and some older Asian guy were in the car. Denise and I got in, and she told me we had to make one stop before the club.

The stop was at a townhouse. We walked in and there were 15 Asian guys probably somewhere between 35 and 50 waiting. I was wearing black pants that were laced in the front, little heels because I'm quite tall, a black see-through top with a red spider web on the side, and a jacket. I did my jacket up pretty fast.

Telling me we were going to the club was just a trick to get me dressed up. The guys were mostly playing cards. We sat down and then, 1 by 1, they approached us. They always made the first move. They would say, "You, in the room." They treated us like chattel. I freaked-out and then they became nicer. They said "please" and "thank-you" after that and they were super-awesome-nice.

That first night I went with 7 of them. The minimum number of guys was 3 and the most I ever went with was 8. There was no negotiating the price. It was a straight 60 bucks. We were expected to have oral and intercourse. It took 3 minutes. It took more time to take my clothes off.

It wasn't that hard to have sex with these guys. I just had to lie there. The lights would always be off, and the few times it bothered me I would think that I could go get Boston pizza after or something. The best part was getting paid. I did it for the money. It took 15 minutes and I would have 500 bucks. Everything else takes effort. I worked at KFC and it was 2 weeks to make 200 bucks.

My best friend Leyla moved in with us in October because she wasn't getting along with her mom's boyfriend. I had already started prostituting before she moved in and I kept doing it. We would go to the mall and eat 20 times and buy sweaters. She would ask me how I had so much money and I'd tell her Carlos gave it to me. Eventually I told her what I was doing and she said, "Oh, we should do that".

When we wanted money, we would call Luu Dang and he would find people. He would pick us up and take us to 1 of 3 places. Sometimes he took us to that first townhouse or somebody's apartment or to another house. At the townhouse there were 2 bedrooms upstairs. They were kids' rooms; sometimes we did it there. I felt bad about that. I saw a photo of this girl and I knew her.

She went to my school, which was weird.

We went to this one guy's place and we did it in his bedroom. His wife had all of her stuff set out in their bathroom. She had hair dye and her little brush, her necklace was by the sink. There was all her stuff and her kids' stuff; there was *Hello Kitty* everywhere.

When Leyla and I would go, there were usually 8 to 15 guy waiting; they were mostly Vietnamese. There was no violence, except once. One of the guys asked me to do it without a condom and I was like, "No way," so he pushed me. I pushed him back and he stopped. I'm 5-foot 9. You don't push me.

I don't know if their wives knew their husbands were having sex with minors, but they know now. Three of the johns were fined, but only Luu got jail time. The fine was only 50 dollars, which is pathetic. It's less than they paid us for sex.

There were a lot of girls involved, but I only personally knew about 9 of them. The youngest was Tabitha. She was 12. Her older sister Melanie got her involved. She was my sister's friend, and she came to our house crying one day because her sister had talked her into having sex with some guy for 1000 bucks, and that's how she lost her virginity.

I guess a lot of girls from my school just started doing it. Everyone just knew that when you needed money, you could call Luu. He did everything. He would call all his friends. He'd pick us up, he'd drive us home. He didn't touch our money, though.

It was easy for me because my mom wasn't around a lot. She was dating that guy at work, so if she wasn't working, she was with him. I was free to do anything I wanted.

I felt like I was expected to be the mom. I would buy my sister lunch at Starbucks so she wouldn't have to make it. I would make her dinner. Then I'd tuck her in, lock the door, and go do my thing. It was kind of fun. My dad left when I was little. I last saw him when I was 5.

*Her aunt pokes her head in and tells Lauren she will be out for the evening and reminds her to unload the dishwasher. A hairless, skinny, gray cat slips in and jumps into Lauren's lap. The cat resembles Gollum from* The Lord of The Rings. *It has a big head and its skin is crinkled and warm to the touch. When her aunt closes the door behind her, Lauren rolls her eyes. She whispers about her cousin Emily and how she is never asked to do anything around the house. She lets the cat out before telling me how she spent her money.*

Me and Leyla went shopping. We went to 7-Eleven a lot, and even though it was only 2 blocks away we'd always take a cab. I took my sister shopping and bought her clothes. We would all get our nails done. I bought about 100 pairs of shoes. We'd get our hair done and tip the guy 30 dollars each. We ate out all the time. Sometimes we would make a fort in the living room and have pizza delivered to it.

Carlos needed an antenna for his cell and so I bought a phone for $250, just so he could have the antenna. Even though he had money, he never bought me anything–not even McDonald's. The only thing he paid for was the cab, if I came over at night. He was cheap and that pissed me off. I broke up with him when he tried to put my head through the bathroom wall.

I bought everything I could think of, and after awhile I just had nothing I could do with my money, but I didn't want to stop because I like shopping and I could go out and make 400 bucks in like 2 hours and I thought that was pretty sweet.

When I think about my experience prostituting, I think I should have bought some better things. Who needs 100 sweaters or McDonalds every day? There were times when I thought, "What the hell am I doing?" But then I was in my shopping phase, so I just bought more clothes.

When I was doing it, I didn't really care. I was thinking about what I was going to buy the next day. What I was going to put on my nails. What I was going to eat when I got home, if we were going to order pizza or get jambalaya fettuccini.

I didn't really think about the sex because it was over in like 2 minutes. Sometimes I was thinking about that, too, and their little pathetic lives, and how their wives must not be happy.

My mom always asked me where the money was coming from. I would tell her Leyla's mom was giving it to us. Sometimes, I said it was from Carlos. A few times I said I found it. I think she knew I was lying, but it's not like she could do anything to stop me. What could she do?

*This is an odd statement. When I press her, she reminds me her mom was too busy with her "stupid boyfriend" to notice much.*

Me and Leyla prostituted from September to December, a few nights a week. That's when we got caught. My mom got suspicious and she started hounding me about how I always had so much money. I kept telling her that I found it or Carlos was giving me money. I guess she didn't believe me because she called the police to talk to us.

The night Detective Wickins came to my house, Leyla and I had just made a fort in the living room. My mom told us that 2 detectives had come to speak with us and I thought it was about the speed we had just bought. We had just done the speed, so my pupils were dilated. The first question he asked me was, "Do you do drugs?" I said, "No. Do you do drugs?" He didn't like that, because he's authority, but I didn't care, he dropped in during my fort time.

He asked me where I was getting my money and if it was prostitution related. I denied everything. He gave us his card and told us to call him if we ever needed help.

A week after he had come to see us, we were at the townhouse doing our thing and I totally freaked out for no reason. I guess I just got really scared because this cop had come to my house. I was paranoid because I thought like maybe he was watching us. Me and Leyla left the townhouse right away and called him.

The next day he took us to the station and we gave him a statement on video. He went to see the other girls who were involved, and that's when Luu got caught. Not everyone was happy about this because some of us were happy with the money and pissed off that Randy ruined everything.

*Detective Wickins says he was shocked that the girls were not grateful for being rescued. "This is an entirely new attitude we're facing, where the girls are telling us to fuck off." He describes the young women as "promiscuous entrepreneurs" who need to be saved from themselves.*

I never thought of Luu as a pimp. He was just a nice guy who was trying to help us, but the cops changed that. Now I think he's a bastard. Randy [Detective Wickins] also told us how we were doing a bad thing and how Luu was just using us. It was only after the cops started talking to us that I started feeling bad about myself. I didn't think of myself as a prostitute before that.

Randy told us that if we went to court, Dang and the others wouldn't be able to see us because there would be a screen up. When we got there, they were standing outside the courtroom and he saw us. We were really upset. We ratted on them. We didn't know what they were going to do to us. We didn't end up testifying because there was a plea-bargain, but they already know who told on them.

I'm not sure what long-term effect this has had on me. I really hate older men. My current boyfriend is my age. I told him about it and he cried, but now he's okay with it. Some people have made me feel badly about prostituting myself. I moved in with my aunt to get away from my mother and my school.

I met Angie, Lauren's mother, a few days after interviewing Lauren. Angie is pretty with large, black eyes framed by perfectly sculpted brows. Her hair falls in thick waves to her shoulder. She asked us to meet her at Lauren's grandmother's house, where the walls are covered with photos of Angie and her 2 daughters.

Angie arrives direct from the hair salon, dressed in a tailored, woven blue jacket, dress pants, and polished chocolate-brown boots.

Lauren is there too. She dropped in to visit her grandmother, but she disappears into one of the bedrooms when her mom arrives. Lauren is angry that Angie is being interviewed. She feels her mom is trying to upstage her by making this a story about something that happened to her. Lauren tells me that when she received an invitation to appear on *Oprah*, Angie pressured her to accept. Lauren declined being interviewed.

In our many phone conversations, Angie has never angled for the spotlight. Once the lights are set up, Angie begins to sweat. Beads form on her forehead and slip over her lips. She tells us it is menopause and asks for a fan, Kleenex, and some hot coffee. After wiping off most of her mascara, she tells us about her relationship with Lauren.

## Angie, Lauren's mother

Lauren and I were really close for many years because I am a single mom. When I got involved with Ron, it was the first time in a very long time that I was experiencing romance again. It was new for me to be taken out on dates; I would leave the girls alone too often. I know they were angry with me all the time because they felt ignored. If things started to happen with Lauren at that time, I didn't notice because I wasn't there even when I was physically present. I didn't notice when there were changes.

She had already started dabbling in prostitution through Carlos, but it wasn't until the problem was quite advanced that I noticed that she had changed a lot. The first thing I noticed was the change in her behavior toward me. In the past when we fought, she would be in my room an hour later asking me to not be mad at her. When she changed, she stopped caring what I thought. I would tell her to do something and she would refuse and be in my face. Before I knew it, we were in way over our heads.

*Angie has a deep, steady voice. She takes a sip of coffee before relating the moment when things tipped out of balance for Lauren.*

When she was 14, she lost her virginity to the popular boy in school, who bragged about it. We did have the sex talk when she was 12 and I did stress to her that her virginity was not just something to be given away, so I was surprised when she told me that she had had sex on her birthday.

After that, all of the boys tried to have sex with her. They began calling her a slut and other names, which was very hard for her. We thought high school would be better because it was a new school, but the summer before she began, she was rebelling and she was very much into boys. When she got into high school, those problems became worse.

I think she is looking for love and that she equates sex with love, but I thought she would be more careful with herself because she had a bad experience the first time.

We assumed she wouldn't be bullied at her new school because she didn't know anyone there, but she told me that she was still being harassed. I guess the kids all know each other and they talk. She began skipping classes and lying to me about her whereabouts. She told me that she was skipping because the boys were calling her names.

I tried to cut her some slack and I spoke to the vice-principal at her school, who suggested that we try home schooling, which was a horrible idea because it requires supervision and discipline. I work full-time and she was too young to manage it on her own.

She became increasingly defiant. She told blatant lies. She stopped doing her homework. She didn't care what I thought or said about her behavior. My husband left when Lauren was about 5 or 6. He calls sometimes, but he hasn't taken any time to be a father to them, so there was no one around.

The first time I found $420 in her purse, she told me she found it behind Starbucks. Listening to her tell this elaborate story, I felt sick to my stomach: I knew she was lying. Lauren has always been sneaky. I call her my sneaky one. We have always been able to resolve these incidents together, but then she stopped caring about how I felt when she lied to me.

It was in December that I became really concerned. She bought me a pair of Fubu sneakers for Christmas and lots of gifts for her sister, but she couldn't explain where the money was coming from. Her best friend Leyla had moved into our house, and sometimes they would tell me that Leyla's mother gave them money.

A few nights every week Lauren would get a call on her cell and they would dress up and leave. I thought that because they were together they were safe. I eventually called Leyla's mom and asked her why she was giving the girls so much money. The money wasn't coming from her; she had been told that the money was from me. We thought they might be drug runners or selling drugs, but we never once thought about prostitution.

I did everything I could with Lauren before calling the police. I yelled, I cried. I invited a social worker to my home to speak to us. None of it made any difference. It was too late. I didn't really know what to do, but I was forced to act one night.

We had had a particularly bad fight where Lauren and I were both screaming at each other. I threw the cup of coffee I was holding at her. She came at me. She threw me up against the wall, slapped me, and kneed me in the stomach. I have never been assaulted before in my life and I certainly never expected my daughter to hit me. I was devastated.

I phoned a crisis line that night and told them that we were in real danger. I explained that I was concerned about the money she had and the dramatic change in her temperament. It was hard to explain what was happening because she didn't have a car and she would be home by 11 or midnight. They put me in touch with a police officer.

Detective Randy Wickins came to my house and confronted them the next day. I didn't know that they were high. I didn't know the signs. I didn't know until recently that my daughter had tried any drugs.

He spoke with them, but they still went out that night. Their routine was to wait for me to go to my room around 8 and then to slip out. They were always home before 11.

My daughter called Wickins a few days after he came to the house. He picked them up and took them to the police station and videotaped their statements. Even after speaking with him, they didn't stop prostituting themselves. I think they wanted to make a few more dollars before the whole thing fell apart.

I asked Leyla to return to her own home soon after we learned the truth about what they were doing. Lauren got really scared when the police began speaking with the other girls who were involved.

It is my suspicion that this prostitution ring isn't dead and that some of the girls have gone back to it and that they are recruiting new girls.

One of my [younger] daughter's girlfriends recently approached her to have sex with men for money. My daughter is still a virgin. Her friend told her she could get a lot of money for her virginity and then she could see where she wanted to go with it. My daughter told me she thought about it for 5 minutes and then refused. The fact that she thought about it at all frightens me.

The next time her friend was at my house for a sleepover, I told them that I didn't want to hear any more about prostitution. I told them that I didn't want them to think they were that worthless.

*Angie did not call the girl's parents and the girls are still friends. She explains that she thought it would be better to monitor her 13-year-old daughter's friend rather than forbidding the friendship or getting her into trouble at home.*

Lauren has gone back to prostitution a few times since the bust. I think she's drawn to it because it's easy. She's all about sex and money. She felt as though she was branded when she lost her virginity and that she can't shake the slut label. I think when you are treated like a sex object, and called names, you believe that that is all you are worth. You have to be a really strong person and know yourself and your worth to avoid getting caught up in potentially harmful situations. But my daughter is like me; she's wishy-washy when it comes to men and she is easily led, at least where it concerns sex.

I am still scared for Lauren because she'll be just fine and then she'll do something crazy. She recently met 2 black men at the mall where she was working and they almost lured her to Las Vegas.

She called me at work to tell me that she had met some guys who were going to hook her up with a great sales job. They were going to get her hair and nails done and make her beautiful. She told me she was packing and that she was leaving with them.

I have never felt such fear. I told her that if she went with them, I would probably never see her again because it was likely that the job was prostitution. I told her she would die out there. I told her that it was suspicious that they wanted to hustle her out of town that afternoon without a proper goodbye to her family or a forwarding address. We were on the phone for an hour before she agreed not to go.

*Angie looks exhausted. As we pack up our gear, she disappears to find Lauren. They emerge arm-in-arm and announce that they are going to dinner. Lauren and I hug goodbye.*

I met Leyla, Lauren's best friend, at her home. Leyla's mother works at a restaurant and her father is in sales. They are divorced.

Leyla is tall with straight black hair held in a ponytail at the top of her head. She has an oval face with darting, shrewdly observing black eyes. Dressed in worn, pink velvet sweatpants and a thin, embroidered top, she is deeply tanned. She unwraps a cherry lozenge.

"I'm not sick. I just like the way they numb my tongue," she says, crunching down.

She lounges on the living-room couch and picks at the clear polish on her nails. "I was making $1000 a week, sometimes more," she says. "At the time I was prostituting I didn't think it was wrong. I just thought it was sex. No big deal. It was just sex and it wasn't that bad for me because I was the one with all the money."

Her younger sister arrives, drops a pink backpack on the couch, and kicks us out of the living room so that she can watch cartoons.

Leyla takes me upstairs, where we sit on her bed among the many stuffed bears and dolls. She opens her closet door and pulls out *SpongeBob* cartoon slippers. She puts them on, plops back down, and holds up her feet for me to admire before relating the events that led her into prostitution.

## Leyla, 16

Grade 7 was the first year of junior high, and I remember being really excited about school. In elementary I had better than average grades, but this year I wanted to get solid A's. I joined the school choir, and that's where I met Trish. Trish's parents were also divorced, so we had that in common.

After school we would hang out at the Boys and Girls' Club and play pool. She was sexually active, so I learned a lot about sex from her. I didn't have sex until I was 13. It was fair. I had a pretty good year at school and things were pretty good until I turned 14.

In grade 8, Trish's older sister, Dana, asked me if I wanted to try speed. She didn't pressure me to do it, but she definitely got me hooked. It was bad. When my mom found out, she put me in rehab for 3 months. I went back to school after I got clean, but it was like everyone knew what had happened, so I started getting into fights with people. I became a mouthy student. The teachers hated me.

My mom let me finish the school year through home schooling. My mom's pretty cool. She let me paint my dresser purple to match my purple bedspread and she bought me these cool green curtains. She also likes a lot of the same music, so we play my stereo super loud and sing the rap and reggae lyrics.

*She slips off the bed and opens the top drawer of her dresser to show me her collection. There are 6 tightly packed rows of CDs. On top of her dresser are photos of her with her sister on a roller coaster and another of the 2 of them at a campsite.*

My dad lives in San Diego. I used to spend the summers with him, but when he remarried, he started a new family. This is the first year that he didn't call me on my birthday. I guess he forgot. It was a month ago and I'm still mad about it, even though he's already apologized 100 times.

*She takes a seat on the bed again leaning against the stuffed animals.*

In grade 9, I wanted to go back to a regular school because it was the beginning of high school. I wanted to experience it. The school was far for me, so in October my mom asked Lauren's mom if I could live with them. Lauren and I have been best friends since elementary. She lived a lot closer to this new school, and anyway my mom and I were fighting every day because her boyfriend practically moved in with us.

I loved living at Lauren's. We had a blast. She had all this cash and we would buy everything. When she finally told me what she was doing I thought I would do it too because I didn't want her to pay for everything all the time.

*I ask her if she is angry at having been recruited, and if she felt she had little choice but to prostitute, since she was living at Lauren's home.*

I wouldn't say that I was recruited, and I don't blame Lauren at all for bringing me in. I earned a lot of money doing it, and that meant I could have more fun. I did not feel coerced. I felt I was there of my own free will and I didn't have to do it if I didn't want to. But I did like it. I liked it because it meant I always had lots of money, and the sex wasn't horrible.

*This is such a curious statement about the sex not being horrible. When I ask her to elaborate, she says, "It just wasn't that bad."*

When we wanted money we would call Luu Dang and ask him if he could hook us up. He would pick us up and take us to 1 of the houses. There were usually quite a few guys there, and sometimes there were girls from our school who were there doing the same thing and we would do our thing.

The guys were all middle-aged Vietnamese men. They were always good to us. They were never mean to us and they never made us do anything that we didn't want to do. The way it worked was, they would approach 1 of us. They'd just stand up and say, "Do you want to come with me?"

We did speed a few times, but we didn't do a lot of drugs. We didn't need drugs to have sex with these guys. It wasn't like that. Sometimes we would have a couple drinks while we were doing it, but we never stayed there to relax and visit. We were there for sex.

*Unlike Lauren, Leyla is defiant and unapologetic.*

Lauren and I didn't do it every night, but just when we ran out of money, which was probably every couple of days. Usually we spent our money shopping, and we spent a lot of money at McDonalds.

Once in a while we would throw a party. My mom would ask me how I had so much money because I wasn't working. She put money in my bank account for clothes and food and stuff, but not like that much. My mom was worried that I was selling drugs. When she asked me where I got the money, I would tell her not to worry about it. I would make up big lies or, if I had a lot of new clothes, I would say that they were Lauren's.

It was after my mom talked to Lauren's mom that she confronted me about prostituting myself. I denied it. She and Lauren's mom spoke to the cops. It was after the cops spoke to us that I admitted everything to her.

It was only when we got to court and talked to some of the other girls that I learned that Luu was making money too. The guys were giving him 40 bucks, which I remember seeing once. I didn't think about it because I thought he was hooking us up to be a nice guy. He would say he was just helping us out, getting us money to shop. I would have cared if I knew he was making more money than us, but I wouldn't have cared otherwise.

At the time, it never fazed me to have sex with so many men in one night, but now when I think about it, I feel gross. I didn't grow up knowing a lot about sex because it wasn't something my mom was comfortable talking to me about.

After my experience with speed, my mom didn't want to put any ideas into my head about other risky things. She believes I have the addiction gene. I don't think she knew that I had already lost my virginity before I ever tried drugs.

I think she should have talked to me about drugs and sex. She should have told me that sex is something you cherish. If she had talked to me about sex, I would have had more respect for my body and myself. I wouldn't have given myself away for money.

The effect of this experience is that I feel lower about myself. People who know about it say, "She's a ho and she sleeps with men for money." That's not how I want people to think of me.

*Leyla stays on the bed and watches me pack up my recording equipment. She adds a final thought before reaching for the TV remote. It was worth it, though, because I had all that money at a young age, and now I have the experience so I'll be more careful in the future.*

Marissa and her twin sister were also involved in the same high school prostitution ring. And, they traded sex for money through another man Marissa calls "T."

Marissa is soft-spoken and articulate. We met for coffee late on a Friday night after her shift at a grocery store.

## Marissa, 15

I haven't done much to my room. It's very messy. I don't have pictures on my wall or anything. The walls are just white. My bed has 4 blankets because I'm always cold. Just 2 months ago, a woman was murdered 5 blocks down from where I live by her boyfriend. We just bought our house and now my parents want to move. My dad works and my mom takes care of my little brother.

People at school are only now beginning to experiment with sex and drinking, but I did that when I was 13. I was 13 and I was getting paid to have sex. At the time, I was like, "Whatever." It seemed like fun. I really now wish that I hadn't done it. When I was 13, I was going to bars. Most people do that stuff when they're 18, but I've done all that stuff.

From 13 to 15, if a guy was interested in me, I would get all stupid. I did a lot of growing up in those years. I regret what I was doing, but I'm glad to be out of that phase. Before this happened, I used to wear sweatpants even in the summer, and then I met some girls and they said I should show off my legs so I started dressing scandalous.

Now, I'm back in sweats only and I stay home on Saturday nights. I'm in grade 10 and I have a lot of homework, so there isn't a lot of time to do much. I will be taking boxing on the weekends, and then I also work.

When I'm not working, I stay home and eat. I don't go out any more. I don't watch TV. I read a lot of non-fiction. Sometimes, I read my mom's romance novels. I received a modeling scholarship for $900, but I don't know about that as a career. Going to school is the hardest thing for me because everyone is so immature.

When I was 12, we met these guys and they were drinking and my sister went with 1 of them. I was trying to go home and this guy offered to take me. I was raped. It was forceful. He still goes to my school and he's friends with a lot of people that I'm friends with.

I got involved in prostitution when I was 13. I met "T" in the summer. He started taking us to the fair and he bought us those big teddy bears. I still talk to him now. He's way older than me, 33, I think. I wouldn't say that "T" is a recruiter or a pimp. He has an image that he likes to portray. He wants to be a big-baller — a guy who gets anything he wants. He drives an SUV with a TV in it. When I go out with him, he'll watch his TV, text message, and drive all at the same time.

When we first met him he was living with his mom. He had a normal relationship with his girlfriend. She would have to be pretty dumb not to know, but he doesn't want her to know. He's got 30 different girls, some he sleeps with and some he's friends with.

When I was 13, I really wanted a cell phone and these sunglasses I saw in a magazine. "T" took us shopping. He has a girl fetish. He took us out to eat. You know how girls want their boyfriends to treat them? He did that. He bought us jewelry.

He never wanted anything. He just said, "I'll hook you up and I'll give you $100 for every guy." If you thought it was too low, you could say so. He knew how old I was and that I was a virgin. He offered me $3000 to sleep with me. That situation made me grow up very fast. He hooked me up with a phone. He wasn't a pimp to me, but he was to other girls. He would just ask sometimes if I wanted to hook up with 1 of his friends.

He tells me now, "Out of the whole thing, I liked you best." We're still friends, but I don't see him as much.

Me and my sister met Luu Dang through Denise. She's not the classiest of people. If she wanted to get picked up by a guy, she'd just flash her boobs at him. She'd do anything. Her family is broken. Her dad died when she was 5 and her mom travels for work. My mom felt bad and took her in. I was really close to my sister, and then my sister and Denise started hanging out.

Denise was prostituting before she came to live with us. She got my sister into it. I don't know if you know this about twins, but we do everything at the same age. The first time my sister drank was the first time I drank. The first boy she kissed was the first boy I kissed – it was the same boy in elementary school.

She and Denise told me what they were doing. I didn't want to do it. My sister slept with Luu and gave me her money. I saw the money they were making. It was a lot of money. Even now, it's hard for me to have a job because the pay is so low. Every week, I was making a minimum of $1500. One week I made $3000, but I have nothing to show for it. I spent my money on stupid, repulsive things. I was so stupid and I would never do it again, but if I did it for a month, I could buy a new car.

When Luu would pick us up, we'd go to this apartment or this really horrible house that had a dungeon downstairs, and that's where we did it. We went every second night. For 2 to 5 minutes I got $100. Blond girls can make a lot doing this. The guys at the house were old, repulsive men. I wanted to throw up every time. These men want to have sex with virgins. These are dirty, old fetishists. I never asked them why they sleep with little girls. I thought that what they were doing was wrong. They had kids our age. Lauren had classes with the daughter of 1 of the men.

The johns were all Asian. "T" was Asian and Luu was Asian, too. Luu never slept with any of the girls except the initial time. He paid us and then he didn't do it again. It was as though you had to sleep with him before you could go with the others.

I bought a lot of stupid clothes with the money. I was dating a 19-year-old guy and he crashed his car and I paid for it. When I was little, material things meant a lot to me.

My mom was suspicious, but we always had an excuse for it. We'd tell my mom that "T" took us shopping, but that we wouldn't do anything with him. My dad never said anything. I don't think he even noticed. He probably just thought my mom was giving us money. My mom told us that if "T" ever asked us to do anything to tell her, and that she would pay him back. I think she knew what we were doing, but she's in denial.

*Vancouver Detective Raymond Payette explained that Marissa's mother's response is typical of that of many parents. "A lot of parents pay pimps off. If a girl resists prostituting, the pimp will sometimes call her parents directly and explain that their angel owes them thousands in clothes or jewelry. They pay up."*

I think my sister took Lauren in and then Lauren started doing it. Lauren took 1 of her friends in. Lauren was coming home with $400 every night. I don't know who brought Melanie in, but then Melanie told her sister Tabitha about it. She told her, "Do you know how much money you can make?"

She was 12 when she did it. She could give a guy head and get 200 bucks. She dresses very scandalous. She doesn't have a curfew. She was making more money than all of us, and then she started getting her little friends into it.

Tabitha told Lauren's sister to do it and Lauren freaked out. Melanie is still doing it. She fucks a taxi driver because he drives her, because Luu can't drive her any more: he's in jail.

Lauren's mom was the one who called the police. When the police took us to the station, I was really scared and crying. That bastard Randy Wickins wouldn't let me call my mom. I kept telling him that I wanted to talk to my mom and he wouldn't let me. I wanted her to come get me.

We told the police that they never forced us to have sex. They didn't need to because they could always find other girls to do it. There are also way more guys doing this than anyone can imagine. They're between 28 and 40. Some of these guys sell drugs, but they're not all low-level. I think a lot of these guys are Asian mafia. It's not over. If we wanted it to happen, it would still happen. A lot of girls are still doing it. There were more than the 50 girls Randy knows about.

"T" told me there might be retaliation against Lauren for talking to the cops. I'm scared she might get killed.

When I went to court, I wore a gray suit and heels. I feel badly that I got involved. What kind of man will want a wife who has done this kind of thing? I got my best friend involved and I feel badly about that. We aren't friends any more: she got pregnant.

I'm trying to have a normal life. Now I realize that my education has to come first. I have 2 part-time jobs. My dad and I don't really talk. We're not the kind of family that says, "I love you." My mom knows everything now, but she doesn't want to talk about it. When I think about what happened in my life from 13 to 15, I feel disgusted with myself. I don't know what I want for myself. I don't know who I am.

# A Real P.I.M.P.

On June 15, 2004, Luu Chi Dang, 35, was sentenced to 2 years in a federal prison for having sex with underage girls.[27] The girls who were involved described Dang as a friend and said he did not coerce them into prostituting. In their statements, some of the girls said he created a "win-win" situation for everyone involved.

Letters of support from friends and family submitted to the court on Dang's behalf describe him as a "caring person," a "great friend with a kind soul." Detective Wickins, who was responsible for the bust, believes "Luu was successful because he was a nice guy. He wasn't violent."

Pimps have become hard to profile. They wear Kappa brand sweats, Louis Vuitton accessories, Puma sneakers. They drive SUVs, and they live in suburban neighborhoods.

Pimps like Luu Dang are nearly impossible to spot. Luu works at a

---

[27]On June 15, 2004, Raymond Shik Chuen Wu, 53; Quyen Tat Tran, 38; Xian Hua Cao, 43; and Phuc Van Co, 38 were charged with unlawfully obtaining or attempting to obtain, for consideration, the sexual services of a person who was under the age of 18. Each of the men received a conditional discharge and paid a $50 fine.

gift shop in Chinatown, dresses Sears-style clearance, and drives his mother's car. He does not see himself as a pimp and claims that he was simply trying to help his married friends who want sex and the girls who wanted money.

I interviewed Dang at an Edmonton Correctional Facility. He is 5 feet, 2 inches with a prison buzz cut and crooked teeth. I thought it would be strange to be in a room alone with him, but he is exceedingly polite. Using phonebooks, he even constructed a makeshift tripod for my camera.

Prior to his incarceration, Dang lived at home with his mother and 6 brothers and sisters.

## Luu Chi Dang

I am Chinese from Vietnam, and I came to Canada when I was 16. I have 3 brothers and 3 sisters. I live at home with my mom and my brothers. I have a very simple life. I've never asked for anything fancy. Life is very simple for me. I dropped out of school after grade 10 because school was kind of tough for me.

When I quit school, I got a part-time job as a dishwasher. My next job was at a pizzeria as a cook. My family has had a gift shop in Chinatown for the last 14 years, and after the pizzeria I began working there.

The way I got involved with prostitution is I met a couple of girls in the parking lot of the West Edmonton Mall. They were in a car waiting for someone, and when I walked by they asked me for a cigarette. I gave them a cigarette and went shopping.

A couple of months later, I stopped to get gas and the same girls were at the gas station. They said they recognized me and asked me for a ride, so I gave them a ride. Then they asked me for my number, so I gave them my number. A few nights later, they called me and asked me to take them for coffee. When I picked them up, they told me they wanted to make some money.

I asked them how they wanted to make money. They told me they wanted to trade sex for money. I asked them how old they were and they told me they were 19. I think, here you have the freedom to trade sex for money if you are 19. They asked me if I had any friends interested in trading sex for money. I called my friends and asked them if they wanted to trade sex for money.

I wanted to help them. I always help people. Maybe it's the way I was brought up. My friends were interested, and finally they did it a few times. Then the girls started to tell their friends, and everybody knew to call me if they want to get hooked up. They always called me. I never called them.

I think it was easy for these girls to trade sex for money because they had done this before. Some of my friends told me some of these girls are still doing it. I've told my friends not to do it because I don't want them to end up like me, in trouble, in jail.

I'm in jail now because when the girls called me I picked them up and drove them to the house and then took them home or wherever. I didn't take advantage of them. Even when I had sex with them, I had to pay. I did not get money from them, not even a penny.

I got nothing from nobody. All I tried to do was make sure that the girls were okay. I picked them up at their house, took them to the apartment or wherever to have sex; I stayed there until they were done and then I drove them home.

When the girls wanted to make money, I would call my friends and say, "We have some friends here — girls who want to make money. Do you want to have sex? If you're interested you can drop by."

It was $60 for each person. It was good money because sometimes it was just 1 or 2 minutes. Most of the girls said they just wanted to make money to go shopping. When their friends saw them shopping they would tell them, "If you want to make money, contact Luu," and I would hook it up, which I did for nothing. I didn't charge anything for that.

Every time I saw the girls they were always happy. The only problem I think is money. They wanted more money for more shopping. A few 100 dollars is not easy to make when you work a regular job.

I also dropped them home before 10 pm. It only took maybe 1 or 2 hours and then they had to go home. It was fast because my friends didn't go there to party. We just went there to have sex.

After the girls got their money, I think they were happy and I think they wanted to take off. They didn't want to stick around. All they needed was money and all we needed was sex so it was really simple.

The girls would call me 4 or 5 times a week. They would have sex with 6 or 7 men each time. Most of my friends were married, some of them have kids, but they were out for fun. We didn't know the girls were 14. If I had known they were that young, we wouldn't have done that: the law here is different, I know. People over 18 can do whatever they want, but not under 18.

I didn't think it was wrong to sell sex, but after I went to jail and heard a lot of people talking about the sex stuff I learned that it's wrong. But we didn't force them to do it. They wanted to do it.

I really think I am the victim here because I was too easy for them. I never said no to them. If they wanted to eat, I took them to eat. When they wanted to go to shopping, I had to take them to the mall. I gave them almost everything they wanted. It was hard for me to say no to them.

Then we had a problem because my friends told me the girls were using the money for drugs, not shopping. I didn't want them to spend money on drugs, so I told my friends we had to stop it. I didn't want them to buy drugs. That's why Lauren got pissed off at me and called the cops on me.

If I didn't pick them up and take them to the house and then drive them home, nobody would. The last time I picked them up, I took them to the house and then Lauren took off. She called me half an hour later and said she wanted $200 from me. She told me if I didn't give her money, she'd call the cops on me. I told her to go ahead and call the cops.

Finally, she did call the cops on me and I ended up here because they're underage. If they'd told me they were underage, I probably would not have done that.

The night Lauren called the cops, the cops stopped me as I was driving home and told me I was under arrest for sex with underage girls. They kept me at the police station for a few hours. They told me that I could not contact my friends who also got caught and charged.

My 4 friends who were charged got really simple sentences. They got a $50 fine and that's all. For me I got 2 years for this and no parole. Everybody did the same thing but I'm only the one in jail. I think those guys got pretty lucky.

When I think back, it seems like I was really stupid. I tried to help the girls and I tried my best for them, but because I wouldn't give her (Lauren) $200 she called the cops on me. I think about that and I think I'm so stupid. I think I am the victim. I feel I am the victim, but I don't know how to describe why.

I never thought of myself as a pimp. If I had taken money from them or forced them to have sex, then, of course, I'm acting like a pimp. But I didn't do that. They did whatever they wanted to do.

*Luu sounds like an accidental pimp.*

My family was shocked when I was charged. They didn't know I was doing this kind of thing. I got shocked in the court when the judge gave me a sentence of 2 years because all my friends got nothing at all. A $50 fine is like nothing at all, but I have to be here for 2 years. It's really dreadful and really scary because I've never been in trouble before and never been to jail before either.

At first I was really scared because I know people use you for sex, but everybody here behaves. I still have 9 months of my sentence to do, but it's been really nice. Since I've been here, I find it's a really relaxing place. You have a lot of time to think about what you've been doing. Jail is like a really nice place.

When I get out, I'm going to go back to work at my family's gift shop full time. I feel bad about what happened. I didn't know it was illegal. If I had known it was illegal, I wouldn't have done that because nobody wants to be in jail. I'm not going to see any of those girls any more, but I heard they're still doing it for money.

All of the girls who did this are white. White girls don't really mind having sex with men for money. They're not like Chinese girls. White girls only care about is money. They don't care about anything else. As long as they make money, they're happy. They don't care about their future. They don't even think about it.

Chinese people get taught from the time they are little; Chinese parents care about what their children are doing. I don't think the parents of these girls cared about them. Sometimes when I talked to the girls, they told me that at home it's not like a family. If these girls had a good family life, they wouldn't come out and do stuff like this.

## Hitting Bottom

Many middle class girls are abandoned by their parents and families when their drug experimentation becomes an addiction and their behavior becomes intolerable. These are often the girls who end up as street prostitutes.

## Greta, 16

Greta performed her first trick when she was 11 at a casino hotel located on Kelowna's waterfront. Kelowna is 5 hours north of Vancouver and part of a prostitution circuit that includes Vancouver and Penticton. Girls who are recruited in Vancouver are trafficked to these 2 cities where they are "broken-in".

I met Greta through a counselor at the safe house where she has lived for the past year.

The safe house is in a suburban neighborhood and looks like a regular home. The yard has a colorful swing-set, a vegetable garden, and patio chairs. The safe house director is on the porch lazing in the sunshine. There is a feeling of calm about the place.

Inside, the walls are golden-yellow and sunshine streams in from the many windows. The words "safe house" take on new meaning for me, as the bars and locks of my imagination are replaced with a cozy setting. Each young woman has her own bedroom and the girls are encouraged to establish connections with each other and the staff, and to develop a sense of family and belonging.

Greta is tiny and dresses in oversized clothes. She offers to show me her room and leads me to the top floor. An unfinished puzzle takes up most of the space on her dresser; the chair by her bed has numerous stuffed animals and a palm-sized red Bible on it.

I give her the care package my mom prepared. Inside are homemade cookies, licorice, a book by Francesca Lia Block that is a fairytale about love, and a few magazines. She eats and reads while I untangle an extension cord and check the sound on my camera.

Starting is the hardest part. Although Greta is articulate and funny, her extensive drug use has caused serious memory loss. She has no recollection of long blocks of time and many of the things that have happened to her. She is adamant that she never had sex for money.

Finally, it comes out that she is afraid she will be judged. "It's just really scary to be on the corner and working at 12 years old. That's just really horrible. I don't even know what to say," she explains.

We stop and start many times. Sweat beads on her forehead. Pulling at the neck of her thick, blue sweatshirt, she excuses herself to change into a T-shirt. When she returns, she is calm and seems steadier.

*I ask her to start by telling me about her childhood.*

My parents divorced when I was 5 and my dad raised me. I grew up in Sarnia, Ontario. I basically didn't see my mom for 6 years. I liked living with my dad, but I really missed my mom, and I didn't understand why my dad didn't want me to see her. I just thought, everyone else has a mom. Why can't I see her? Sometimes when she would call me I would cry because I missed her so much.

When I turned 11 my mom asked me if I wanted to live with her in Kelowna. My dad didn't want me to go. He said it was too far away from him; he said he was worried I wouldn't have any friends and that it would mess up school. I didn't care: I just wanted to be with my mom. He basically gave me an ultimatum that I could go and live with her or I could live with him. He told me that he wouldn't have anything more to do with me if I left.

Living with my mom and her boyfriend was just a little weird: there were people coming and going at all hours.

At my new school I became best friends with Lily, and we would smoke pot at the back of the school or in the alley behind the 7-Eleven. Then I gradually started drinking, and then I tried hash, then mushrooms and acid. I was having a good time, so I didn't care. I guess somebody noticed and Social Services came in and took me away. A month after moving in with my mom, I was put in foster care.

I was really mad about being taken away from my mom, because all this time, all I wanted was to have my mom. I started running away to go look for her, and that's when I started getting mixed up with prostitution.

I started going to where all the hotels are and I met this girl and became really good friends with her. Her mom was into drugs, so I'd hang out with them and smoke pot, drink.

Then I met Raven and I started spending more time at her house, and her mom was pretty cool. She asked me if I wanted to try crack. It was an intense high. I would take a hoot and it would last 3 minutes, then the comedown would be really horrible. You need more right away because you feel so bad. I started averaging a quarter ounce a day. That's a lot of drugs. I'd do $500 worth every second day.

One day her mom told me that it was my turn to pay for the drugs, and when I didn't have any money, she told me I would have to go to the street. She told me how to do it. You just stand out there, wait and stand. A car pulls up and you go up to the car and you ask them if they want any company and you just get in the car.

I saw these girls and watched what they were doing, and then I began imitating the way they walked and what they said. I started wearing slutty clothes and putting on thicker, darker makeup. I started to get picked up. It was fun. I started working to pay for my drug habit, and I guess it just got worse and worse from there. I got addicted and started working all the time.

It was fun for a while and it was easy. Cars would pull up and they'd ask me how old I was. I'd say I was 16 because I was 12 and they're not really going to believe my age.

Some of the johns knew I was 12, but they didn't care. There are a lot of men who want sex—grandfathers, dads—regular people with wives, with kids. Most of them asked if they could have the pleasure without a condom. Sometimes I would do it without because they would offer more money. I don't know why they would do that because they could get sick. I guess they just didn't really care.

Some of the johns would ask me why I was prostituting. I would tell them I was here because I had nowhere else to go. I remember working on the streets at 3 in the morning waiting to get picked up, doing drugs behind this convenience store.

I moved in with my mom again when Raven and her mom moved away. I went home and I told my mom that it was better for me to be doing drugs in front of her than behind her back. I used that excuse on her. She agreed with me. I guess I just didn't see that it wasn't right. We began using together.

My mother's boyfriend went to jail for dealing. My mom started prostituting to pay for her drugs. Because a lot of the guys were people she knew, they would come to our house and that's how I would meet them. They would come to the house for her and then they would see me. I think they were really coming to the house for me, and she knew and she didn't care. She was pimping me out to these guys. All I wanted was to find my mom, and this is what I was introduced to – drugs and   prostitution.

Sometimes they would go with her and then they'd ask for me. We were sharing the same customers, and that's just horrible. I thought that was really horrible. I didn't think that was right. I hated it. I hated the lifestyle.

We kept doing it, though, until my mom developed cocaine psychosis.[28] She was paranoid all the time. It was horrible. I couldn't even do drugs with her any more. I didn't know what to do, because when I moved in with my mom, my dad told me that he didn't want to have anything more to do with me. I called him anyway and he came and got me 2 days later.

My dad got me into rehab, but I didn't make it the full 7 days. I only made it 4 days. Being addicted to heroin and crack is a really hard thing to overcome. My dad didn't understand. He just thought I could do it if I wanted to. He was mad at me all the time. I couldn't take it. I told him I wanted to go back to my mom, so he bought my plane ticket back.

I lived with some friends, went back to the lifestyle. It wasn't like I was making that much money. I would go down there and make $40 dollars, feed my habit, and keep doing that.

I don't remember how I got out, but I wanted to get out because I want to have a normal life. I can't really describe normal to you, just without drugs. I've always known I can get help. I've always had these resources, but you need someone who loves you to make it. There are people who can support you, like safe houses and counselors, but you have to want it. If you have the

---

[28]Cocaine psychosis includes symptoms of aggression, paranoia, and hallucinations of insects crawling on the skin.

will to want to be clean, then you can do it. I don't think you can do it without someone who loves you.

My boyfriend is 34 and he's got HIV. I get tested all the time. He's really careful because he doesn't want me to get it. He's helped me a lot. Since coming here, I've only relapsed once. I'm now 5 months clean.

My mom still lives in the same city as me, but I can't see her. I blame her for what happened to me. I was just a normal kid, and all I wanted was to be with her, and this is what happened to me. I don't want to end up like her. It's a really lonely, sad, destructive road to go down.

I have someone in my life who really loves me and I have found God. Having God in my life, everything seems easier.

Allison has curly, sun-bleached hair, thick lashes, and large blue eyes. Dressed in a baggy white T-shirt and blue jeans, she is comfortably reclined on a couch in her drug and alcohol counselor's office in Nanimo, BC.

## Allison, 15

My mom left when I was a baby. My dad said she couldn't handle having a baby. She's never called me or tried to get in touch. My dad works 2 jobs, so he's not around a lot, and then when I turned 12, he became really strict with me and my sister. He wanted me to stay home after school and on weekends and study and I didn't want to.

I was 13 when I met Kevin. He would hang around our school. I thought he was really cute, so I went over to his house after school one day. I had never done any drugs. He came in with a pipe and he asked me if I wanted a hoot. I thought it was pot; it was crack. I got addicted really fast.

We hung out a lot, and at first I thought he was great. I felt I belonged with him. He was so nice to me. He actually listened to me and took notice of the things I was doing and how I felt about them. He was 24. My dad didn't approve. We did a lot of crack, and then he just stopped giving it to me.

When I told him I wanted more he told me, "There's a guy you can get money from and then I'll give you more." There was a guy who wanted girls for money, so I went over to his house and slept with him for money and kept doing that. Basically, that's how it happened. I was 13. I wanted the drug and I wasn't thinking.

I thought Kevin wanted to be with me forever and that we were going to have this great life together, but it didn't turn out that way. He started getting abusive. He started hitting me.

My dad didn't know I was prostituting myself. He kept sending the cops to look for me. I got busted by the cops, who said they knew I was prostituting. When they took me home to my dad, I told him I didn't know what they were talking about. I lied. I kept doing it. My dad would ask me how I had money and I would say my boyfriend gave it to me, and he would get mad and call me a whore.

I broke up with Kevin when I met Trevor a few months before my 14th birthday. He introduced me to heroin. After I met him everything got way worse, the using, the working. He was beating me. When my dad found out I was using, he didn't want me at home any more. He said I was a bad influence on my sister. I had nowhere to live and so I moved in with Trevor, and he put me on the street.

The guys that were picking me up were beating me up. There are a lot of guys who want to have violent sex with small girls. I thought I deserved it because of what I was doing. I didn't have anyone. I had dropped out of school. A typical day was: I'd go out, get money, get crack, and do it. I wouldn't sleep or eat for days.

I told Trevor that I didn't want to be on the street anymore and he stabbed me in the back with a small knife. He was ripping my clothes. I think he wanted to kill me when his dad walked in and saw what was happening.

He took me out of there and brought me to see a nice lady who was a drug and alcohol counselor. That's when I started getting help. She told me that what was happening wasn't right. I didn't realize that—someone had to tell me.

I struggled with the drug use for about a year. I went back to it and the working a few times, but I've been clean for 6 months, almost.

I'm happy now. I'm happy now because I can sit here and not think I'm disgusting. Every day now I wake up and I go to school. I work on my life. I try to help other people.

My dad never told me about drugs. I didn't know about cocaine or heroin or crystal meth, so I didn't know the effects of those drugs. If my dad had paid more attention to me, I think he would have noticed and gotten me help. He's there for me now. I guess he wants to help me because I have goals now.

Vicky is tall, thin, and very pale. Her aquiline features accentuated by penciled lips and eyebrows. Her ears are pierced all the way around and decorated with red and blue studs. She is wearing fashionably ripped and faded jeans, a

T-shirt, and green Adidas sneakers. She and Allison are friends.

# Vicky, 15

I met Kim in grade 5 and I started hanging out with her after school, and that's when I met these Asian guys. She partied with them and asked me to come along. There were always a bunch of us who went, so it was fun.

Some of them were really great guys, and some of them, you know, they just want to have sex with you. My friend told me she had done it and they bought her whatever she wanted. It sounded really good. If I'm going to sleep with one of them anyway, why not get paid for it? Right?

Once you do it, there is nothing stopping you from doing it again. You get to know all the guys. They buy you whatever you want. When I was 12, I was making 300 bucks every Friday night. I thought I was so cool. When you've got that much money coming in every few days, all you think about is going to the mall and getting a new outfit. It felt good not having to ask my parents for money.

I would go shopping and buy jewelry and eat at all these places. I had money in my pocket, why not go out and spend it? I was addicted to the money, starting to get addicted to drugs, and even the sex gets addicting. I mean, me and my friends were hanging out with these good-looking Asian guys. I found these guys attractive. If you find somebody good-looking, it's just like being with any other hot guy, right?

I started doing it more after school and on weekends. I would tell my mom I was going out with friends; she had no clue. I would sleep with 1 of them and get 100 bucks. Wow, 5 minutes and I got 100 bucks. I was meeting other girls through them who were doing the same thing: high school girls who do it, but don't tell anybody about it.

I got more into it when I started partying more. It was around then that I stopped doing normal stuff: I didn't go to school dances or anything like that because I was too busy doing this stuff. We'd go out and party and 1 of my friends would say, "This guy wants to do something with you and I'll give you this much money for it." So I started meeting more guys and doing it more.

It was fine, but then they started adding more and more guys, and then you have to do it more. I didn't want to make them mad and I wanted the money to go shopping, so I did it. I also started doing coke. I was smoking it, snorting it, shooting it. Then I started using heroin because it would make me feel better from the coke.

Lots of the Asian guys we hung out with were older. We partied with the younger Asian crowd too, but it was the older Asians who were married and had kids who we did more shit with because they're married, they can't really go out and party.

When my mom asked me how I had so much stuff, I told her my dad's girlfriend was buying it. My mom and I would fight, but there was nothing she could do. And then my mom met this guy and she kind of just said, "I'm moving to an apartment building that doesn't have kids, so you have to live with your father."

I tried living with my dad, but that was horrible. I wasn't allowed to go out or do anything. So I started running away and hanging out more and more with these guys. What other ways are there to get money? If you're doing drugs, how else are you going to get money?

Some of my Asian friends knew somebody who had a house in Vancouver where girls worked. If you're pretty and you're willing to do the work, there's always someone there to give you work. I was 13 when I started (and I worked) until just months ago.

I also worked at a massage parlor. It was fun when I was at the massage parlor and making almost 1000 bucks a night. It was degrading when I stopped to think about it, but once I got the money in my hand that took care of everything.

When my friends found out I was working there, they were really good guys and they didn't want me doing that so they had me selling coke instead. They found out I was starting to use, so they cut me off completely. I went to the street.

When I was on the street, most of the guys were disgusting. It's not like *Pretty Woman* at all. There's no sympathy when you're out on the street. They don't look at you like you're a kid.

I didn't get help until I almost died from an overdose. It had happened before, but this time I woke up and nurses were stripping me down and doctors were telling me that my lungs had collapsed and that I had an infection. I think it was when they wanted to stick me in the psychiatric unit that I pretty much decided to get help. You have to want help, and I wasn't ready for help for a long time.

I'm back in school now and living with my dad. I'm just taking it a day at a time. I do have a lot of hatred toward guys, but I think I'll be able to have a good relationship with a guy one day. I hope so. I want to get married and have kids.

# Conclusion

**What to do if you suspect your daughter is already at risk**

The police liaison at your daughter's school will be able to direct you to the unit dealing with child prostitution. "If we suspect a girl is being targeted by a pimp, we'll provide a timeline which plots the events leading up to the point where she will turn her first trick," explains Detective Raymond Payette, Vancouver Vice. "Then we show them where they are on that timeline. We predict the future for them," Payette explains. "Some girls tell us to fuck off only to come back for help when they recognize what is happening."

Ask the officer for the name of a youth counselor at an addiction prevention center. As well, ask the officer to recommend an agency that works with street prostitutes. The counselors will know of resources for teens.

Act quickly. Pimps are linked to organized crime. According to the Polaris Project, an organization combating human trafficking, approximately 200,000 American children are trafficked into the sex industry each year.

Girls in the United States and Canada who are drawn into prostitution and lured away from their families are domestically trafficked. Popular trafficking routes follow music festivals like Lollapalooza. "We've found the music festivals to be popular with pimps. Girls are made available to fans and musicians," explained Detective Payette.

## What To Do Now to Help Your Daughter Avoid This Pitfall

There are many steps parents can take to help a girl on this path.

### When you are with your daughter...

**Communicate.** The best way to keep your daughter safe is by being a good listener. If you know what is happening in her life by taking a regular interest in what she says about her classes, friends, and projects, you will send her the message that you care and that you are a resource she can turn to in times of trouble. Being an attentive listener will also help you to identify changes in her behavior.

**Do not be afraid to assert authority.** While your daughter is a teenager, you are the authority figure in her life. Although there needs to be room for her to negotiate for the things she wants, teens equate love with safety. Denying your young daughter's request to walk to the pizzeria alone at night tells her that you care about her safety. Saying "No" in a kind, gentle manner, and occasionally with a touch of humor, will show her that these boundaries are inspired by caring and meant to protect her from harm. Your daughter might not thank you for keeping track of her whereabouts, but it does not matter. Your teenager needs to believe that you see yourself as her parent and not as her friend. If you demonstrate that you have good judgment by making sound decisions for her, she will turn to you when she is in trouble. Teens have very clear ideas about good and bad parenting. She will not turn to you if she believes you are too permissive, a pushover, or simply do not care.

**Don't give up.** I have a teenage nephew, and for the last 3 years, we have spent part of every summer together. Inevitably, we have some kind of disagreement over the house rules, such as going out alone after dark. If he does not like one of my rules, he is quick to slip away and call his mother to get permission to do whatever I just forbade him to do. He will emerge from the other room to inform me that his mom says it is okay if he goes skateboarding at 9:30 pm and out he goes. These episodes used to really upset me. Was I wasting my breath? No. You should set boundaries for your child, after listening thoroughly to their point of view and input, and stick to them. Even if you discover that your child is doing an end-run around your limits, do not assume that your child has not heard the message of your values. Sit down again, talk about them again, be willing to bend if you sincerely believe your earlier rulings were in error, and stick to your decisions. If you accomplish nothing else, you at least send the messages that you listen and you care. The value of these boundaries, for young teenagers, is also being able to say to their friends, when they find themselves in uncomfortable situations, "I want to go with you, but my mother would kill me!" instead of "Sure, I can stay out all night–I don't even have a curfew!"

**Help her to discover and develop excellence.** Young women who believe they are skilled athletes, dancers, writers, painters, singers, piano players are less dependent on external approval to be happy. They can identify many aspects of themselves that are valuable, powerful, and praiseworthy. In addition, the energy and discipline required to excel at these things allows a girl to develop her ability to focus and concentrate. It will show her that she is capable of mastering difficult tasks and setting goals for her future.

**Praise her.** Tell your daughter that she is intelligent, perceptive and insightful, on a regular basis. Praise her on her ability to write stories, complete challenging math questions, and her skill at conducting science experiments, even when she struggles with these things.

**Help her to see her best self.** Help her to develop a strong self-image, and she will do her best to live up to it. Tell your daughter that she looks like: a runner, a dancer, a hockey player. If she is shy and sits on the sidelines when other girls play sports, encourage her to participate by telling her that she has the body of an athlete. Too many of us allow our self-image to be determined by the media. Her friends can also determine how she feels about herself and what she believes she is capable of accomplishing or becoming. Teach your daughter to surround herself with a cheering section of friends who encourage each other.

**Assign chores and duties.** Your daughter needs to become aware of her own capabilities and her ability to meet challenges. This can start at home, with taking responsibility for household chores and duties. From the time she is young, ask your daughter to help make dinner, clear the table, or sweep the floor. Her chores can increase in responsibility as she gets older and more capable. By expecting your daughter to help you, you show her that every member of the family is required to contribute to the household's well-being. Perhaps more importantly, she will feel a genuine sense of accomplishment. Self-esteem comes not from being told how capable we are, but from experiencing first-hand our own ability to meet challenges and rise to them.

**Stack the rafters.** Imagine a basketball game where the stands are stacked to the rafters with, encouraging, trusted adults. This is an adult cheering section for your daughter. These are the people from your extended family, community, church, and neighborhood that your child can turn for advice and guidance. Support from outside the immediate family is particularly important at times when she does not want to talk to you.

**Spend time.** Fathers who do not develop strong relationships with their daughters by the time they are 12 might not have that opportunity again for years. Even if your child is miserable about having to spend her weekends with you or your family, tell her that you will take her however she comes; let her know that you want to spend time with her even if she is sulking.

**Don't forget touch.** Hug your daughter. As teens get older, they shy away from being touched by their parents, which means that it can be weeks between hugs. Physical affection -- in the form of hugs, play wrestling, brushing her hair -- is important to a girl's emotional well-being.

**Be a shining example.** In the movie *Spanglish*, Flor, a single mom, is with her daughter, Cristina, at a restaurant when 2 men at the bar send Flor a drink. She refuses the drink and asks the waitress to tell the men that they should be ashamed of themselves. "Can't they see I'm with my young daughter?" In doing this, Flor is showing Cristina that it is not necessary to be flattered by all male attention, that male attention or the promise of romance is not superior to female company, and that she need not become available simply because a boy shows interest. We all learn by osmosis, by example and by doing.

**If you find yourself in conflict with your daughter...**
Wait to react. Do not meet aggression with aggression. Assume that your daughter will become calm, if you are calm. It is hard to yell at someone who is not yelling back at you. By doing this, you model the behavior you expect from her, and show her that there is a way to meet conflict calmly and reasonably.

**Apologize.** A young friend of mine told me that her father had apologized to her after a misunderstanding. I was stunned. I did not think parents ever apologized to their children. The trust and respect earned from the gesture of an adult apologizing to a younger person will be immeasurable in her mind.

## Talk to your daughter about...

**Drugs and alcohol.** Alcohol is used by children as a rite of passage into adult life. When you talk to your daughter about drinking and drugs, she needs to know what you stand for as a parent. Do not reminisce with her about your wild and crazy days, as this gives her permission to emulate your behavior. It also makes you a hypocrite, in her eyes, if you try to stop her.

**Sex.** Even if you do not believe in pre-marital sex, you need to find a way to communicate your values while also talking about the possibility of a relationship that includes sex before marriage. Tell her what a relationship that includes sex would look like. This will help her to develop expectations and not just settle for whatever is offered. Help her to see that an intimate relationship requires open communication, trust, and friendship. If you are unable to have regular and meaningful conversations with your daughter about sex, public health nurses are among the best people you can turn to for help. Without your active participation, graphic depictions of sex on the Internet, questionable information from her peers, and pop culture will form the basis of your child's sex education.

**The value of intimacy.** Too many parents are letting their kids down by not having meaningful conversations or providing role-modeling that shows them the value of intimacy. The media have shifted our perception of what the true meaning of sexuality could be for an individual or in a relationship. Our concerns about disease and pregnancy have prevented us from helping teens to celebrate their sexuality in a way that is meaningful, significant and a beautiful thing for the rest of their lives. We also socialize girls to use their sexuality and charm to get the things they want. Tell your daughter that she can afford to pay her own way and that it is cheaper to pay her own way than to trade her body and her dignity for dinner, drinks or clothes.

**Expectations.** Assume your teenage daughter will be offered drugs or be pressured to have sex. Does she have the skills to extricate herself from difficult situations? Or, will she simply go along because she got caught up in the moment and did not know what to say? What are her expectations for herself? If she believes that the first time she has sex it will be a beautiful experience, it probably will not happen in a public bathroom. If she believes that drug use will kill the brain cells she needs to be sharp on the ice during hockey practice, she will be able to tell her friends as much. If she knows what to say to a boy who is pressuring her for sex, she will not hesitate to remove herself from his grasp. For example, "I'm not having sex until I'm at least 18."

**And perhaps most important of all…**

**Love.** Girls give themselves away because they are desperate to hear the words "I love you." Tell your daughter that you love her, every day. There is no substitute for saying or hearing the words.